Last Days in Naked Valley

LAST DAYS IN NAKED VALLEY

The Struggle for Humanity's Homeland

EDWARD DeMARCO

ISBN 979-8-218-02808-4

Afrologi Media LLC

Cover design and interior design by Susan Kisangau, Forte Digital, Nairobi. Photographs by the author.

To Renée and Lara,
who took me there

Contents

1

Leaving Ethiopia

STARCHY, CIVILIZED ETHIOPIA rolls to a stop at Arba Minch, delivering your first triumph over the enigmatic national tongue known as Amharic: welcome to Forty Springs. Lush with palm-frond flora and breezy sapien fauna, Arba Minch affects a relaxed, anything-goes vibe, a tropical tonic for life in the uptight, pious north.

Ethiopia's youth hordes tumble into a final pileup here, proof that Africa's most populous nation after Nigeria, 2,000 miles to the west, exudes a passion to propagate. Almost half of Ethiopians are younger than 18 years, about 50 million youth in all. Like pilgrims parting a sanctified darkness, students from the university stream down into Arba Minch at night, illuminated only by their glowing phone screens. As they crowd the cratered roads, vehicles bearing outsiders bounce past, climbing to a high point.

Sunrise brings forth shimmering revelation. While the forty minch remain concealed and thus somehow mythical for the casual visitor, liquid smooth and sloshing glistens the daytime scene. From the terrace of the Paradise Lodge perched on an escarpment at one end of town unfolds one of East Africa's most sublime panoramas. Two mighty Rift Valley lakes come together, separated by a narrow hump of land known as the Bridge of God. To the left one admires the milk chocolate expanse of Lake Abaya, while a pivot to the right brings smaller, darker Lake Chamo into view.

Dimly perceived, about six miles across Chamo's waters, festooned with ravenous Nile crocodiles more than 12 feet long, sits lonely Nechisar National Park, named after the white grass of its desiccated plain. Thousands of zebras roam there today, a remnant of the varied beasts driven or hunted out in past decades of political upheaval. Like cousins of *Madagascar*'s skittish stars, the wild residents of Nechisar fled into exile with predators at their backs – in this case marauding Marxists.

A visitor to Paradise relaxing on the lofty terrace one day in August – a rainy, cool month in the highlands of Ethiopia – would have paused with his glass of trembling beer suspended in the fading afternoon light as an odd spectacle hummed into view.

A craft smaller and quieter than an Ethiopian Airlines turboprop, workhorse of the domestic aviation fleet, had risen from Arba Minch's diminutive airfield, soaring past Paradise, climbing above the Bridge of God and a dense, darkening forest below. A winged, windowless tube accompanied by a distinct whirring sound. In a few moments, the mysterious machine banked sharply to the left, heading east for the battlefields of Somalia.

Leaving Arba Minch is the beginning of leaving Ethiopia. Yes, the political map still places you firmly within the sovereign bounds of the federal democratic republic, latest incarnation of a stubborn and secretive 3,000-year-old nation once ruled by divine, and sometimes divinely maddened, kings and princes. Chilled beer and warm injera, Ethiopia's spongy, slightly sour mealtime staple concocted from the grain teff, will still be found down the road. Donkeys will reliably meander into your path and cattle may clog the roadway. Yet settled, highland Ethiopia waves farewell from Forty Springs, as the road snakes down the escarpment and makes its way toward the Konso lands to the southwest and eventually into the great and enveloping valley of the Omo River, where time itself drifts away.

The word Omo occupies a magic space in the mind of the highlander Ethiopian, for few have visited that far-off land. They will know pictures of women in braided, ocher hair, oiled breasts dangling, or lips stretched to grotesque lengths, or men resembling birds with hair feathered and fancied with red-mud plaster.

These mesmerizing images illustrate tourist ads, promotional videos, and storefronts in the city like come-ons for half-beast, half-human grotesques at a county fair in America. In this spectacle live people of supposed primitive mindsets, close to the mud, devoted to their cattle and guns, enthralled by strange, earthy rituals. Habits like requiring teenage boys to scamper naked over the backs of bulls to prove their manhood. The Valley of the Lower Omo is the other world that modern-feeling Ethiopians file away, possibly while scratching their heads, as they go back to Orthodox Christian and Muslim observances and five-year economic plans and social-media updates. Who are these people that time abandoned and what are we to do with them?

An American boy of the polyester 1970s, living in an era before the world was knit in a tangle of voices and a torrent of instant images, would have asked the same. Opening a National Geographic or an anthropology textbook to ogle fantastic humans like these was glossy proof of an exotic world untouchable and perhaps unreachable even in the era of moon shots. Earth indeed was a planet of many worlds. And this world and its people were decidedly naked.

The highlander Ethiopian, on the other hand, is rather devoted to her garments. The land rises above 8,000 feet and brisk winds blow through the valleys. This is Africa's Switzerland minus crisp ski runs and precision chocolate, an enthralling high-altitude land: the roof and water tower of Africa. In rainy season all is consumed by mist and fecund-damp growth.

Tanzania lays claim to Africa's highest point, Mount Kilimanjaro, yet that cherished summit is a chubby, 19,341-foot-high oddball dormant volcano bursting from an elephant-studded plain. Ethiopia for the most part is majestic upthrust. Waves of rock roll from Arba Minch and its environs to the border with Eritrea hundreds of miles away in the far north of mesas and red-rock vistas. Up there you expect to spy a cowboy charging across the frame kicking up a dust plume of horsepower.

From northern Ethiopian vistas the lofty land tumbles down to the eastern desert out of which lava gurgles and spits from otherworldly Technicolor pools less than 100 miles from the Red Sea.

In those remote, high mountains men may wrap themselves against the chill in a thick, nubby cotton cloak known as a *gabi*. Women will wear skirts of dark green, a uniform of the devout Amhara peasant, and may bear crosses tattooed on their foreheads. In the growing towns and cities of the central plateau, by contrast, T-shirts and jeans sheathe the urbanite. Slim young women, aware of their allure, gravitate toward tight skirts and slinky jackets according to the vibe. Skin may be revealed inside a dance club, yet on the street modesty prevails.

Yet let us spin our compass southward once more, for our journey leads that fateful way. Less than two hours out of Arba Minch, you stop for coffee in Konso, a town set amid terraced hillsides, and perhaps buy a Konso TV (delightful hand-drawn paper channels that unspool as you turn tiny bamboo rollers; the Obamas feature in one). Even here the unexpected may ruffle

6

the calm.

Near Konso once, during a return journey from the Omo Valley, a deranged local hurled a rock at our moving vehicle with the force and velocity of a baseball pitcher, spidering the windshield with a terrific gunshot-sounding impact. A split-second difference and the projectile would have brained the driver through his open window. Yet fate was entirely on his side; the driver had commanded a battle tank in the border war with eccentric Eritrea and thus reacted with cool decisiveness. In 20 seconds, he halted the vehicle, leapt out into a crowd, collared the sullen culprit, and shoved him into the back seat for delivery to the Konso police station.

After Konso the road rolls toward a dramatic valley backed by a mountain wall. One's mind expands along with the vistas, which begin to stretch for long miles toward hazy horizons. The air grows warmer as you descend. As you round bends in the road, children appear, dancing or holding aloft wooden AK-47s for sale. Along the route, clothing begins to fall away.

Young men stand along the roadside without shirts, and soon too their pants shrink, revealing weathered legs though nothing pendulous – yet. While the youth may toss a checkered cape over his shoulder as he displays a few trinkets, the fabric is an afterthought. Young women hint at going topless, with T-shirts straining. It will get a bit steamy out here today. While lips, hair and body art will attract their blinking shutters, the long lenses of the tourists are coming for the bare facts. Make no mistake. The clothesline descent toward the Omo Valley intoxicates with Stone Age titillation. There are rumors of European tourists secreted in Indigenous villages, throbbing with wild dancing, dazzled by the jeweled dome of night.

Before the highlander Ethiopians fully appreciated the untamed potential of the surging Omo waters, the tourists had alighted upon the passions of the pastoralists. With cameras and fat wallets they were turning the valley into a human zoological park. Bagging lenses as the sun dips, they roar off in Land Cruisers to drinks and dinner. You will run across these tourists en route to the valley at a charming lodge in the heights of Konso with a broad view from its stone-floor overlook toward the distant, sparkling watershed of the Segen River. The Segen is a mere stream when compared with the mighty Omo, yet valuable to parched herders wandering the precious grasslands out near Kenya's most remote terrain.

At dinnertime, American, British, and German tourists mingle with aid workers and visiting doctors and nurses volunteering time. The Omo trail is rarely crowded and retains a flavor of exclusivity as if a portal is beckoning into an African Shangri-la. While small, organized tours haul most of these visitors into the valley, independent travelers do venture in. A couple from Los Angeles lingered one morning over breakfast, explaining their plan to wander into one of the last strongholds of deep-time

Africa. A territory patrolled by muscular warriors cradling AK-47s and shadowed by suspicions.

Pastoralist ancients still afoot in these parts seem to regard the land as boundless, or as boundless as their prehistoric needs dictate. Their world of human interaction is bounded, at the service of elemental and recurring facets of life in a natural state. The 21st century Ethiopian nation-state presents a contrasting template: marking off the land into its political and economic uses and unbounding life's consumer possibilities flowing from these utilities. A fracturing of ancient cultures in the march of earth movers, a growl of modernity that the state's men insist heralds rescue from backward ways. "Competing paradigms," we called it in our report from my first foray into the valley.

"The various tribes of South Omo have distinct and ancient cultures, usually based on an agro-pastoralist and mobile lifestyle," said we envoys of Ethiopia's major international development funders, governments American and European. "The Government of Ethiopia's development plans for the region are based upon sedenterized and irrigated agriculture which it believes will greatly alleviate recurrent food security problems; a new departure for cultures whose livelihoods have remained unchanged for centuries."

Or thousands or tens of thousands of years, who knew? Troves of hominid fossils and some of the earliest tools crafted by human ancestors have come to light in the Omo around 4-million-year-old Lake Turkana, which juts into southern Ethiopia though resides mostly in Kenya.

These tools are "evidence of the oldest known technical activities of prehistoric beings," the United Nations explains in justifying designation of the Lower Valley of the Omo as World Heritage terrain. The discoveries, opines the world body, render these lands "one of the most significant for mankind."

Hominid feet have pressed into this soil for what by our mortal timespans is eternity, perhaps a billion days. Time so elongated into the slanting equatorial sun as to transport us onto another planet altogether, the future so remote from those early bipeds that their present jogs in place, refusing to budge. We must whoosh forward like star voyagers into our time, our Earth, to arrive at the political map drawn by the latest evolution of human society on this much trod terrain: the Ethiopian revolutionary democrat. As a revolutionary, he's rather reluctant; as a democrat, he's a flawless fabricator.

Landlocked Ethiopia is divided into 10 regional states, some the size of countries (Amhara, the Ethiopian homeland in the north, is bigger than Bangladesh), and two city-states, the modern capital Addis Ababa, meaning New Flower, and the old French railway terminus in the east, Dire Dawa, pronounced "Dray-da-wah" by highlander Ethiopians. Each state is split into zones that comprise districts known as woredas. The woreda is the basic administrative building block of the country, equivalent to a county in the United States. This political map roughly matches the ethno-anthropological one – so a woreda may capture the core lands of an Indigenous community such as the Dassanech along the Ethiopia-Kenya border near Lake Turkana.

Ethiopia's highlander-dominated government rules the Omo lands – or more accurately, attempts to rule them - through district administrations parceled out among the native inhabitants. Ethnic federalism they call it, a creation of the Ethiopian People's Revolutionary Democratic Front. And many of the administrators are drawn from the modernizing local ancients. They have made the transition, draped their skin in modernity, and grasped fragments of fabric and consumer civilization.

In the lower Omo, land and landscape overmatch people. In the central and northern regions of Ethiopia, villages abut villages, and these turn into ramshackle towns stuffed with jumbled little shops and dark, shabby cafes, maybe a hotel with lousy plumbing. These are pockets of hope. Poverty tumbles among people in proximity to an urbanizing area, according to economists at the World Bank who study patterns of migration and economic promise.

Impoverished Ethiopia often means isolated Ethiopia – distant from roads, stores, knowledge, health care and all modern conveniences, lacking car or bus, squeezing a living from the tired and often thirsty land though with few prospects for rising above subsistence. The farther one gets from Arba Minch, the more one sinks into a sublime though perilous emptiness.

We move out from Konso territory. To reach Jinka, outpost of highlander Ethiopian power as capital of South Omo Zone, one must first descend into a basin that cradles the Weyto River. The approach reveals yet another glorious scene – a lovely green patch at the base of an imposing mountain wall. The green is elusive like a mirage and dazzling from a high, distant viewpoint.

Only when your vehicle descends to the floor of the valley do you realize that this is a farm, of cotton, stretching away to the south. This cultivation is the first sign that waters of this sculpted terrain might carry some mystical property, might infect men with grandiose desires, might shake the landscape from Paleozoic slumber. And we haven't come yet to the majestic Omo River itself.

One of the mind-rending revelations encountered in Ethiopia is the utter mismatch between the musty impression of the place as a bone-dry purgatory for starving peasants, a tumbleweed graveyard, and the teeming water resources apparent in almost all corners of the republic apart from the arid Somali east.

The so-called Blue Nile begins its journey from Lake Tana in the northern state of Amhara and after a long, arduous trek nourishes Egypt. Not so fast, the Ethiopian planners say. With an Italian contractor moving the dirt and pouring the concrete, the Ethiopian revolutionary democrats have built a mile-wide plug 10 miles from the Sudan border in a design resembling a stepped

Mayan pyramid.

The Grand Ethiopian Renaissance Dam, costing five billion dollars, harnesses this branch of the Nile before it escapes to Cairo, and generates electricity for sale to neighbors. Ethiopians rallied to their monolith with messianic fervor, investing their wages in bonds issued by the government to pay for this epic expression of revolutionary development greatness. The rulers in Cairo grow troubled in an existential way, in the manner of inheritors of a sun-drenched great civilization, as the Ethiopian tap settles into place.

The reservoir behind this river wall spreads to three-quarters of the size of Lake Tana, itself as big as America's Rhode Island state, creating a major water feature on the map of Ethiopia for the first time in eons. More surprises await. West of Lake Tana, the road drops below an escarpment so lush it resembles cliffs in Hawaii, opening onto a bucolic landscape of crystalline streams and lovely forests. This is Benishangul-Gumuz state, which embraces the natural flow of the Nile up to the mega-plug.

The simple Gumuz people, more Sudanese than Ethiopian, balance loads on shoulder yokes as they stroll past stunning fairways, dogleg par-5s and rolling par-4s, a golfing paradise. If only there were golf, golfers, golf balls, architects, and tamed earth. One day the Ethiopians will discover how many Europeans they can lure across the Mediterranean with a cleverly positioned golf green and a beer cart steered by a local beauty.

Water replenishes savvy farmers too. Rains that fall hundreds of miles away on south-central Ethiopian fields yield a bumper crop of corn and wheat, enough that those farmers can sell their surplus to the humanitarian relief agencies for hungry mouths elsewhere. Where the land falls off from the highlands toward the east and bolts for the Indian Ocean the earth is indeed dry and sparsely populated, poor and austere. Only one in 16 Ethiopians perseveres there.

For months of every year the vital core of Ethiopia is wet, more Seattle than Sahara. As a friend steeped in the soil reminds me, more precipitation falls on the red-rock terrain of northern Ethiopia in a year than soaks London. The precipitation simply comes in torrents than in steady offerings, and slithers away before humans can detain it.

The Omo River, as we shall see, is perhaps most prized of all as gravity herds its waters down through cascades of southwestern Ethiopia and on to Lake Turkana. Three dams interrupt the descent. In its last stretch before emptying into Turkana, the Omo tours a landscape warm and wide, fertile ground the local ancients used to farm in modest plots as the flooded river receded. Outsiders notice that the black cotton soil clings to boots. They also take note of what this Omo-bathed land loves today: sugarcane.

Muscle and stubbornness that only the 21st century could muster would change the course of the river and its people. The

Valley of the Lower Omo would become an agricultural stage worthy of imperial ambitions in an age without divine kings. In lands where human ancestors may first have chiseled implements to tame their surroundings and improve their harsh odds of survival, a new epoch of land, water, and sugar was taking hold. Yet the existential contest was still very much in play.

2

Our Man Molloka

AS THE DOOR SWINGS OPEN from a cramped, paper-stuffed reception area, you step into a crisp, elongated chamber for executive action. A space embraced and studiously copied like the sacred dwelling of an ecclesiastical brotherhood. For it is here that Ethiopia calls the shots.

A conference table for visitors and subordinates extends from the bigwig's desk to form a solid T. The government's man (and the man is 99 percent of the time a man) can thus hold forth at the head of the meeting, top of the T, without deigning to join the other participants. Behind him or on a wall nearby hangs a photograph of the Great Leader, the imperial M. That Meles no longer draws earthly breath is of little consequence. His exhalations and exhortations still supply the atmosphere from which the governing mortals suck their inspiration.

Emerging from the bush in the era of Bush - the Elder, when

the rusty Iron Curtain ripped asunder and heartless communists fled soulless posts, Meles resuscitated an Ethiopian state whose hopes and coffers wheezed near empty. The wreckage exposed wounds physical, economic, and psychological: a miasma of exhaustion. As the global Cold War ended, Ethiopia awoke from a 17-year Marxist nightmare of collective farms, curfews, ornery orthodoxy, famine, torture, massacre, revulsion, weeping, propaganda, and stark store shelves. Loyalists of the strange regime led by Colonel Mengistu had slain or starved hundreds of thousands of their countrymen, thousands of them students.

In the worst days of the blood-splattered regime, people were executed in the daylight streets in the style of gangsters, according to witnesses. Rather than consolation, devastated families received bills for the bullets.

Faced with the stifling embrace of the state, Ethiopians wriggled loose and voted with their feet. Thousands with the money or opportunity ran away to America, Canada, or Europe. One man walked from the north into Sudan and ended up settling in Israel. When I encountered him decades later in Gondar, a northern town where Ethiopian royals once ruled from crenellated stone castles, he had returned as an Israeli diplomat to bring out the last Jews of Ethiopia.

As the Cold War chill receded, withered pages of Ethiopia's 20th century history wheeled in the warm, fresh breeze. The antique Emperor Haile Selassie, escorted from his palace and stuffed into a Volkswagen Beetle at the start of the madness in 1974, was dead. Vanished too were his eccentric royal court, feudal constructs, and fairytale uniform of starburst medals. The Lion of Judah, for a half-century the most famous African astride the globe, defiant victor over a fascist aggressor, Time magazine cover star, Kennedy confidant, and hero of African independence strivers, saluted only in memory and yearning.

Enter Meles, an action hero with the incisive intellect of a world-class sociologist, alive with ideas, visions, and boundless energy. Just a few years after guerrilla fighters sporting Afros and plastic sandals seized the levers of power in Addis Ababa from the Colonel's dejected army, and following the autocrat's exit to Zimbabwe, the Great Leader made Ethiopia whole again. In time Ethiopians became less fearful, even encouraged. Meles devised Big Plans, courted the rich powers, fed and schooled the children, and sized up the balance sheet of natural bounty. (Upon Meles's passing, technology titan and philanthropist Bill Gates, the world's richest man, praised him as "a visionary leader who brought real benefits to Ethiopia's poor.")

Ever poised to seize emerging opportunities, Meles had squeezed in a master's degree in business administration from a British university. In his liberated land, Meles the management guru found much to work with, especially water. Tumbling and churning from great heights, a cascade of untapped wealth surged onto the national balance sheet.

Egyptians know too well the value of Ethiopian water. The Blue Nile, or Abay to the Ethiopians, emerges from Lake Tana, an emerald inland sea in northwestern Ethiopia. Monks ponder ancient mysteries on forested islands out in the middle of Tana, while on the lake's southeastern shore, an epic sojourn begins. In its first few hundred yards, the Blue Nile doesn't look like much – just a lazy channel meandering from an outlet in the lake, a soothing panorama for a glass of merlot or chardonnay.

Yet over the extent of its travels, the Blue Nile eventually accounts for as much as 90 percent of the Nile waters that flow past Cairo. (Ethiopia contributes another source of the Nile's flow from a river known as Tekeze that rolls down from the highlands on the Eritrea border.) The White Nile, running up from Lake Victoria in Uganda, meets the Blue in Khartoum, Sudan, for the great whitewater trip to the Pyramids.

The Blue Nile gathers volume and majesty as it rolls toward Sudan, propelled by the gradual drop from around 6,000 feet in the highlands. Indeed, one of the river's gaudy early spectacles is a waterfall a few miles from Lake Tana called Tis Abay or "Great Smoke." While Ethiopian tourism posters depict Tis Abay as a thundering, misty water show comparable to incomparable Mosi-oa-Tunya (Victoria Falls) on the Zambezi River in southern Africa, in dry season the Ethiopian cascade is reduced to twisting threads of airborne river. Tourism posters are always freakishly well timed.

After the spritzy gymnastics, the Blue Nile settles back into a lumbering flow, winding in a big arc running from southeast to northwest on its way to join the White Nile, though not before smacking into Meles's grandest ambition just a few miles from the border with Sudan.

Less known though steeped more deeply in human history than the Nile is the Omo. It rises too in the highlands, then cartwheels south toward Kenya through canyons, before emptying into Lake Turkana in the lands of the Dassanech people. The Omo's journey is about 400 miles, a fraction of the Nile's epic meanderings toward the Mediterranean. The Omo's fate is that of the nomad, restless and obscure.

Lonely, contemplative, and romantic in its own way, the Omo wanders far from Africa's crowds. One of my favorite images of the river shows a young girl, her back to the camera from a high vantage point, gazing upon the dark, solemn flow below as it ribbons a vast plain fringed by distant mountains. The image could be from today or a hundred centuries ago.

Upon Meles's unexpected demise at age 57 after an illness, images appeared all over Addis Ababa of him in various guises. One made him look like the cranky uncle of a *Flubber*-era Walt Disney film, a tam-o'-shanter crowning his noggin, spectacles slouched on his nose and shielding a mad stare. By far the most appealing image was this: the young, bearded revolutionary in the bush, bent over his writings, aglow with the dream. Meles's chosen successor, an academic technocrat of limited vision and no romantic guerrilla mojo, or credibility of any sort from the warrior north, instantly became an invisible man. His portrait, even his name, were nowhere to be found in government offices, town squares, airports, taxis, buses, schools, or shop windows.

The message, transmitted through ethereal dimensions from high party realms, was as clear as the rays slicing through the chilly mists of the Amhara highlands. If you want to know what the plan is, you must consult Meles – still very much alive if no longer quite so animated.

Fortunately for the government men charged with the social re-engineering of the Omo time machine, Meles had left quite clear instructions. In Jinka for Pastoralists Day at the start of 2011, the Great Leader described how a 370,000-acre sugarcane development would emerge along the lower Omo once the river was tamed by an 807-foot-high dam, taller than that grand gamble called Hoover outside Las Vegas in the great American desert. Italian and Ethiopian engineers were constructing Gilgel Gibe III about 300 miles southwest of Addis Ababa, jamming a wall into a canyon. Workers were pouring 6 million cubic meters of concrete for Gibe III – about two and a half times the volume of stone in the Great Pyramid at Giza.

Downstream, the ancient, free-roaming cattle enthusiasts would get parcels of irrigated land to till out of the deal and be steered toward "modern cattle herding," Meles disclosed.

Meles lamented that less visionary folk had thrown obstacles in the way of his ambition to give pastoralists a sweet taste of the modern. "There are some people who want to block our freedom to use our rivers, and to save our people from poverty," he told the crowd. "They are creating huge propaganda, and they don't stop there. They are blocking us from getting financial loans from abroad to finish the project. There are also some people who are the best friends of backwardness and poverty but claim to be concerned about environmental conservation."

"They don't actually do anything tangible," Meles pressed on. "They just want to keep the pastoralists as a tourist attraction and make sure no development happens in pastoralist areas. They team up with the people who don't want us to use our rivers, to broadcast their propaganda."

In the gospel of Meles, a flood of nature would be harnessed to market demands. Land, water, and sugar – these were the ingredients of the Omo's new epoch. Yet a wave of human labor and enterprise was soon to inundate the landscape too, a wave the locals couldn't glimpse on the far horizon. The shadow of ambitious Ethiopia was drifting into the Omo Valley, darkening the vault of creation.

The best of the government men that Meles molded fancied themselves as acolytes of his style – earnest with a bit of puffery, answering questions in list form as if delivering a lecture on pesky hygiene habits or urgent political philosophy. Action memos and reports and phone messages demarcated the desktop of the local Ethiopian administrator. Minions darted in from dim, disheveled hallways with guidance or to receive instructions, supplicants parked in the vestibule to gain an invitation to the T, mobile phones bleated with news, directives, gossip.

Ethiopia's victors, the tenacious Tigrayan guerrilla band of which Meles was the international face, could not rule on their own credentials. The people of Tigray make up only six percent of Ethiopia's population and their homeland is situated on the arid frontier with Eritrea hundreds of miles from these lands of the south. Even the language of Tigray sounds like a faraway tongue, reminiscent of Arabic. The Tigrayans knew that franchising their ideology into scores of local markets was the savvy managerial move.

The Omo presented peril and opportunity for the Tigrayan hierarchy, for the highlander face of authority needed to be packaged in the visage of the native aristocracy. Yet in the view of the regime, these natives needed a good scrubbing and a wardrobe update from paleo designs.

As eyeballed by Addis Ababa – governed is too strong a judgment – the Lower Omo Valley was most prized as a national stage for mastery over nature. From vast fields an economic showstopper would yield a triumph of Ethiopian stubbornness over natural-world persistence. And to achieve all this, nudging these pastoralists into a new age became a high priority, even an imperative.

The photogenic pastoralists tended to roam the landscape without reference to the imaginings of the government agricultural architects. Or regard for the sartorial standards of the central planners. The men that Meles made abhorred bare skin. Men, women, boys and girls in these parts tended to eschew the threads that government planners hoped would spin from new factories, possibly drawing on thirsty cotton grown right from the earthy waters of the Omo or its tributaries.

Body art beats buttons. Bare breasts bounce brazenly. The kiss of sun is enough to wrap one's sinewy loins. And the soil is no alien medium for human interaction. In the Omo, getting down and dirty is all about the seamless connection to earth, cattle, sun, rain and ritual. Green yet not altogether clean.

"We cannot assure that the Mursi will continue walking naked," said Ato Molloka one day at his T, around which were seated American and European visitors who represented the major development aid givers to Ethiopia. The Mursi, oft photographed, were known especially for the clay plates that stretched women's lips to stupendous lengths, forming a kind of mind-bending platter. With plates removed, lips dangled pitifully from their mouths.

Molloka Wubneh Toricha. Even now, years later, the nameplate positioned at the front of his desk, at the very nexus of the T, rattles around my brain. No one ever called him all that. To us as Ethiopia's benefactors, to his subordinates out in the valley, to the elders of the Mursi, Bodi, Hamar, Dassanech, Nyangatom and others, he was simply Ato Molloka, Ato being equivalent to Mister or Sir, though in a loftier sense. More like Master.

A short, compact man, Molloka enchanted with disciplined charm seasoned with a hint of menace. Molloka would acknowledge points from interlocutors with a gentle grunt, and go on scribbling notes, before taking a pause, sizing up the room, and launching into a response that could roll on in waves of entreaty and exasperation. While Molloka always welcomed you to his administrative zone, you weren't ever sure that the zone he ran welcomed you.

At what point and by what instigation Molloka had emerged from a village of his Maale people on the eastern edge of the valley to tug on pressed pants and golf shirts for audiences of Europeans and Americans, none of us knew at the time. Perhaps he had been the clever kid who discovered ways for less nimble-minded chums to do his bidding and made handy connections beyond the village.

Officially Molloka was chief administrator of South Omo Zone of Southern Nations, Nationalities and Peoples Regional State, or SNNPR in Ethio-speak. A political scientist once observed that this carnival-tent title bore a strong resemblance to stirring monikers for ethnic republics in the heroic Union of Soviet Socialist Republics. During the mid-1980s famine, Soviet military cargo planes had supported the surreal Ethiopian regime in hauling hundreds of thousands of villagers from the drought-stricken north to settlements in the south, where they found themselves in a tropical African vision of Stalinist collective farms. That kind of heavy-handed coercion was one big reason we were snooping around the valley to see how the locals were getting along.

SNNPR was like a microcosm of the Ethiopian conundrum, a mosaic of around 20 million people into which all manner of human variation was gathered: scores of ethnic groups, speaking about the same number of languages, lived within the state's borders. The people of the far south, of the Omo, were the most exotic, stubborn, endangered – and naked – of all.

In affectations and air of authority, Ato Molloka was more like one of the country's regional-state presidents – bearing in mind that some of these states were the size of countries – than the administrator of a collection of Indigenous lands sculpted by a great river. While remote from the Ethiopian capital, South Omo was no mere appendage of the nation. Rather, here was the heart of Ethiopian ambitions in the far south, intended home for the country's biggest agricultural achievement. A project so bold and sprawling that the Italian occupiers of Ethiopia in the 1930s, who dreamed of building an African farming colony, would have recoiled *con stupefazione*.

Ato Molloka hinted that he often reported directly to the party heavyweights in Addis Ababa. If I'm not here, rest assured you will find me at the table with the deciders in the capital, he seemed to convey. The grand ambition of Meles, the majesty of all that sugarcane, the sheer scale of land and water, motivated Molloka's sense of mission. Yet jostling the Omo Valley's inhabitants out of their timeless reverie and into the Ethiopian future always meant something deeper for him. "As a government we have a responsibility to change these people," Molloka would say, with utmost sincerity.

Any official visit to South Omo began and ended in Molloka's office, tucked into a guarded compound down a quiet side street in the rough and raw town of Jinka. A grassy field cut through the heart of jumbled Jinka like a green scar, a remnant airstrip that anthropologists and other visitors had used decades ago to fly into this isolated region. No flights winged this far south now; Jinka was almost the end of the line before the desolate drylands extending to the border with Kenya and beyond.

While the government lavished attention on South Omo, not everyone in town idolized the government's men. During a visit we heard of a protest being organized about the sluggish progress in building a road, and soon after, security forces clamped down on entry roadways. Jinka was too far from real Ethiopia for such tactics to cause much of a stir. Apart from an odd electronic board for coffee prices set up at an intersection by the fancy commodities exchange back in Addis Ababa, little about Jinka seemed likely to flicker on the outside world's radar.

Still, Molloka made sure during one of our visits to have a regional television crew show up at his office. The images would confirm to his constituents that their administrative chief could gather the country's top sources of international aid around his table for weighty conversation. The zonal czar also was trying to counter the bad press he was getting.

International activists roiled the Internet with reports and testimonies alleging that the local ancients were being rounded up and hauled off their lands, beaten, raped, and in some instances killed, all so the highlander government boys could lay their hands on prime land for agriculture. Among the most vocal foes of the Ethiopian plans was the California-based Oakland Institute, which reported that 170,000 indigenous Omo peoples from 10 ethnic groups lived in peril along or near the Omo River. "As the government's plans for industrial plantations in the Lower Omo have taken shape, they accompany an aggressive resettlement program targeting the local populations," the institute asserted, referring to sugarcane as well as palm oil and cotton growing. "The Ethiopian government claims that the plantations and the resettlement are unconnected yet it is clear that to establish plantations the local people must first be removed from their land – this is the primary purpose of the resettlement."

Ethiopian officials vehemently objected to this conclusion and insisted that their plans were respectful and patient – even, in Molloka's telling, downright progressive by the standards of wrathful regimes of yore. Yet with such accusations afoot, it was the job of the major governments collectively giving billions of dollars each year to Ethiopia – the United States, Britain, European Union, Germany, Canada, and the Netherlands, principally, and even the tiny yet influential Republic of Ireland – to find out if the Valley of the Lower Omo indeed was where Ethiopia's henchmen were clearing the terrain of its iconic inhabitants.

Human rights resonated back home, especially in European capitals where lawmakers could summon aid bureaucrats and render harsh judgment about treatment of the local populations – and their own taxpayers. The British, facing human rights lawsuits, had grown especially jittery. Though Americans might be able to find their neighborhood Ethiopian restaurant blindfolded, the air fragrant with *tibs* and *shiro*, they scarcely could locate Ethiopia itself on their mental map. Africa seemed a messy world away. By comparison with Europe, the pressure from America registered as slight, at least for a time. Yet Ethiopia watchers stalked the corridors of American power too, as my colleagues and I discovered upon waking one day, when a consequential legal entanglement rocketed in from Washington.

On more than one occasion, Molloka railed against the online onslaught though with less enthusiasm than the attacks might invite. In a country tied up in knots over dissent and access to information as the planet exploded in an insurrection of everyman's opinions, Molloka seemed frustrated by his limited means to challenge the haters on slippery free-speech turf.

On Ato Molloka's turf, no such difficulty intruded. Around Molloka during any visit to his dominion gathered a cast of characters emblematic of the Omo's transformation. Sitting along the wall beside the T or strolling the fields of a sugarcane plantation or a Bodi village alongside Ato Molloka would be his security chief, carrying an automatic weapon, with a handgun strapped to his leg. Nearby one would find the administrator of the pivotal Selamago Woreda that hosted the huge sugar footprint, known with tropical levity as Ato Banana. And joining the group were the smooth, English-speaking publicist for the Ethiopian Sugar Corporation and the chubby, Spanish-speaking pastoralist relations head from the regional-state capital.

The heavyset guy was *muy* fascinating. Like other brainy Ethiopians in Marxist days, the specialist had been sent to study in Cuba, a place where sugarcane thickens luxuriant in the humid, socialist rays. I once spotted a vehicle from the Cuban Embassy parked at Ethiopian Sugar's headquarters office in central Addis Ababa. (The Ethiopians also had the Cubans to thank for sending thousands of young soldiers to repel a fearsome invasion from Somalia in the 1970s, with Soviet arms and generals in the background.)

What you would not find in Molloka's office were any half-naked representatives of the groups that laid ancestral claim to the lands of the Omo. Elders in a Bodi village, another people devoted to cattle, told us that Molloka made them walk home, more than 60 miles, after they brought grievances to his T in Jinka. He would hear none of it, they said.

Nor would Molloka mingle with anthropologists who studied these peoples, for they were seen as activists standing in the way of progress, more interested in preserving backward ways than basking in sugarcane-filled glory days. Meles had said in Jinka that he wouldn't allow the people of the valley "to be a case study of ancient living for scientists and researchers."

Whatever concerns the world had about these lands and the cultures rooted in them, intellectual curiosity halted at the skeptical doorstep of the zonal administrator. Wayward, naked intransigence couldn't secure an appointment.

Evangelism was Molloka's favored approach, or at least how he described his relations with the natives. If the Mursi or the Bodi ignore the government's entreaties or sly threats, what then? "We will convince them," Molloka would say in a sharp retort, as if he were speaking about herding philosophic bovines. We feared that this convincing might have a persuasive dimension involving more than hard looks and tough talk.

Ultimately the algorithm of this dispute centered around land – who controlled it, how far one might roam upon it, how free were one's cattle or one's descendants' cattle to graze across it, how untouched might the terrain be from roads and other intrusions, where would water come from and what might life be like were the land to slip away into the state's great farming schemes.

Yet something of the Omo Valley never faded entirely from inhabitants who doubled as stewards of Ethiopia's most cherished agricultural dream.

One day Molloka took us to the immense new sugarcane fields planted in the far west of his zone, the golden lands kissed by the graceful Omo itself. He paused to take in one field, squatted down, balancing his backside, and held steady, gazing into the distance. In that moment he seemed transfixed by the land, back in his natural element, a son of the Omo Valley.

3

Mad About Sugar

WHERE HAD ETHIOPIA CAUGHT this fever for sugar? That tale arises in a distant land and time, an alien mindscape entangled in the obsessions of empire and the crushing burden of colonialism.

Sugar enjoys a light-hearted renaissance in our time, yet from the Caribbean to Asia in past centuries, dark history flowed through these pale crystals. In the drama that would one day unfold in Ethiopia, a small trading nation whose merchant fleet crisscrossed oceans would play an outsize role.

Today the enterprising people of the Netherlands bask in a reputation for peaceful intercourse with their world. Rotterdam is Europe's busiest port. The Hague is home to the International Court of Justice. And Amsterdam offers guilt-free hedonism to a visitor after he exits that solemn shrine to a teenager's defiance of tyranny, the house and refuge of Anne Frank.

The Netherlands pursues humanitarian ventures widely; one of its most daring charities was born to save Vietnamese boat refugees from the war-ravaged 1970s. It has gone on to difficult work in Sudan's blood-soaked Darfur region and in remote borderlands of Ethiopia traumatized by communal conflict. That charity goes by the Dutch acronym ZOA, short for *Zuid Oost Azie* – South East Asia.

"The biblical message of reconciliation and restoration of this broken world is our inspiration," ZOA explains on its web site. "We serve victims of violent conflicts and natural disaster, offering signs of hope and recovery. Our goal is for people to experience peace and justice and eventually regain mutual trust and personal dignity."

Score that as a startling role reversal in the league of redemption, for the Dutch once specialized in turning peoples of the Asiatic tropics into miserable beings. In 1825 a Javanese prince named Diponegoro fomented a rebellion against the overlords of the Dutch East Indies, what today we call Indonesia. Diponegoro quite reasonably objected to land grabs by the wayward Dutch and the dreadful labors these chilly, ice-skating northern Europeans demanded from sweat-streaked peasants to feed their vast trading empire. A guerrilla war ensued, forcing the Dutch to send reinforcements as the locals gained strength.

As in so many episodes of Indigenous indignation, however,

the backlash fell short, and the thrashing followed. When the Java War ended in 1830 with the prince's capture in an episode of colonial trickery, the East Indies became a "subdued province," as Amsterdam's Rijksmuseum gently describes the outcome. The Dutch turned to transforming their twisted paradise into an export plantation for indigo, coffee, and sugar to satisfy European tastes. Perspiration, exhaustion and dirty, scratchy, life-sucking toils ensued, wrapped in batik.

The Second World War and American victory finally broke the Dutch grip on this exotic archipelago. Following the defeat of Japanese occupiers, another homegrown rebellion took hold. This time the winds of world history blew at the backs of the freedom fighters.

Led by the longtime nationalist agitator Sukarno, Indonesia declared independence in 1945, prompting a four-year fight with the Netherlands for control of the sprawling Muslim nation.

In early 1949, American diplomats pondered how to deliver the news to an ally: the game was up. The acting United States secretary of state sat down with Dutch officials and ever so politely informed them that American disgust with the Netherlands' resistance to recognizing Indonesia's independence might force a cut-off of postwar aid. The strong-arming worked. By December, following talks with the Netherlands, Indonesia became a sovereign country. Within a few years the Indonesians elevated their star by hosting a legendary conference to welcome other newcomers. It happened at Bandung, set amid volcanoes and tea plantations south of Jakarta.

In Bandung, Asian and African nations, including Ethiopia, announced their arrival in the new world order, rattling the established powers. "The seizure of power was not on the agenda; Bandung was not concerned with how to take power," recounted the American writer Richard Wright, who attended the unusual summit and delivered his impressions in a book, *The Color Curtain.* "All the men there represented governments that had already seized power and they did not know what to do with it," Wright reported. "Bandung was a decisive moment in the consciousness of 65 percent of the human race, and that moment meant: How shall the human race be organized?"

Sukarno's triumph marked an early blow against European colonialism, and the Dutch obsession with sugar worked by Indonesian hands soon began to fade. A major grower, Handelsvereniging Amsterdam (HVA), set sail for distant fields across the Indian Ocean. The Dutch ended up in East Africa about 70 miles from Addis Ababa near the Awash River. On 12 June 1951, the Imperial Ethiopian Government granted HVA a lease on 3,705 acres of land on the Awash in the Wonji plain near Nazareth with an option on 8,645 adjoining acres, for producing and refining sugar. The Ethiopians agreed to a 60-year deal, renewable for a further 30 years, giving HVA sugar output potentially into the 2040s, a century after the world war that had triggered the Dutch downfall in Southeast Asia.

HVA agreed to build a factory to process at least 500 tons of cane daily into 40 tons of sugar, with the aim of producing about 8,000 tons of sugar annually. "HVA has right to use waters of the Awash River for irrigation," the Ethiopian Ministry of Commerce reported to American officials. "Development of the concession to date is eminently satisfactory."

The Dutch settled in for the long haul. They built a cozy community, transplanting a mid-20th century vision of European-American comfort onto the hardscrabble template of rural Ethiopia. Ranch-style homes sprouted on a grid of tree-shaded roads. Nearby a social club catered to homeward longings. Decades onward, the homes remain in what seems like a moldering time warp, a decaying museum to misplaced suburbia. The tennis courts at the club are cracked, and the restaurant soldiers on in fine 1950s style.

Only the sugarcane remains fresh, still nurtured by waters channeled to the fields in canals. Ethiopia fell madly in love with sugar here and never looked back. Over time came the Ethiopian Sugar Corporation, designed to put the state's imprint on the sugarcane bounty in fertile fields elsewhere in the country. What the sugar daddy appeared to engage in was squeezing sweetness from cane for cash. In truth the parastatal harvested water, for *Saccarum officinarum* is a notoriously thirsty crop.

While Ethiopia's resilient farmers rely on rainfall to grow

teff, coffee, wheat, sorghum, maize, and vegetables, and suffer when the sun scorches the land instead, Ethiopian Sugar depends mostly on irrigation from rivers. No flowing water, no crystalline goodness in your bowl. Rainfall helps yet isn't enough to slake the thirst of skyscraping cane arrayed like an army on the march.

The water requirements of sugarcane are 1,500 to 2,500 millimeters evenly distributed over the growing season, according to the Food and Agriculture Organization of the United Nations. In one gulp, that's equivalent to as much as eight feet of water. Sugar content at harvest is only about 12 percent of the cane's fresh weight. From another angle, almost 90 percent of the vegetation fashioned by all that water and sun and nitrogen-rich soil never makes it into your fizzy-sweet drink.

Temperatures around 90 degrees Fahrenheit help sugarcane thrive. In Ethiopia you must descend thousands of feet from the highlands to around 1,400 feet above sea level find that kind of warmth day in and day out. By the early 21st century, Ethiopian Sugar was casting its gaze to the southwest, to a great basin near Kenya through which meanders the Omo River, giving sustenance to native populations of pastoralists. Their prized possession is cattle, free to roam the grasslands that roll out in vast yet increasingly crowded terrain. When the Omo swells with the inundation from the highlands and later retreats, the pastoralists plant sorghum in the rich soil on the river's edge. Sorghum supplements their diet of milk – or cow's blood.

We rumbled into this basin one November day in 2012, admiring the solitary mountains to the west that framed the view into lonesome Omo National Park. The United States, European Union, Ireland and United Kingdom, we were – better known as Edward, Emma, Peter and Paul, a pop group of dubious vintage. Colleagues from the German and Netherlands embassies joined us for the trip.

In a photograph from that week: Peter, a beard beneath his cap and looking like he's headed to an Irish village pub; Paul, beefy in a solidly British way and earnest of gaze under his white baseball cap, toting papers in a transparent sleeve; and Emma of the EU, her golden-haired head wrapped in sunglasses and reaching only to Paul's shoulder, a tight grin blossoming.

The washboard road here crossed one of Ethiopia's most remote stretches of terrain. The only other vehicles leaving Jinka with us each morning belonged to the handful of tour companies taking Europeans or Americans in for thousands of dollars apiece. They would never see sugarcane.

The road wound down an escarpment, affording massive views from the forested cliffs southward toward Kenya. We seemed on top of the world. At the bottom one entered the broad plain of Mago National Park. A stream marked the border between Mursi and Bodi territories. Eventually we rolled into the muddy frontier town of Hana. Hana was so much at the fringe of this outland that I once picked up the satellite-phone network for Kenya at one end of the town and the network for Ethiopia at the other.

Men wearing toga-like garments mixed with youth in T-shirts as construction vehicles rumbled down the mud-slick main street. Shops and rough-hewn restaurants punctuated the roadway leading toward the plantation. When an old rugby injury flared up to perturb Paul, a local man offered up his staff so that Paul could make his way in Hana. A meal of suspect tibs – Ethiopia's classic cubed beef sauteed in a spicy concoction – hobbled the rest of the team.

From our Land Cruisers bumping along the main construction road leading from town, we strained for glimpses of the river. Instead, a muddy channel about 50 feet wide dominated the scene, still being dug parallel to the natural watercourse. Ahead the road climbed emphatically toward a prominence overlooking the basin: headquarters for construction of the Omo Kuraz Sugar Plantation, the greatest agricultural project in the millennial history of the Ethiopian empire and one of Africa's boldest manifestations of land and water. Ethiopia was investing as much as two billion dollars in this basin. If built to government plans, Omo Kuraz would stretch south along the Omo's course, sweeping through Indigenous pastoral lands and skirting – or possibly invading – the Omo and Mago national parks. In its path, the native Mursi and Bodi in the north and the Nyangatom in the south would give way to mega-scale agriculture.

Cane would crowd more than 300,000 acres, possibly over 400,000, an area as big as 15 Manhattans. In return, the government promised plots of land for small-scale farming and grazing land for cattle – plus access to health care, schools, and clean water. The bargain, assuming you were willing to park your herd, sounded trendy and exciting, as did the term coined for the marketing drive: villagization. Escape your Stone Age troubles, economize and villagize, where the living is easy.

Thousands of scattered Ethiopians had already fallen into line as the scheme played out elsewhere in the country. In the lush Benishangul-Gumuz State hundreds of miles to the north alongside Sudan, the forest-dwelling Gumuz people were clustering into communities near new roads. Health posts and schools were cropping up nearby, along with shops, giving the Gumuz a taste of modern amenities and opening new routes into Ethiopian society. I had visited Gumuz communities and shouldered one of their yokes with baskets at each end to feel how much weight they balanced while walking long miles through their countryside. Life here, as in many parts of Ethiopia, still demanded an abundance of grit and physical endurance.

In the Lower Omo Valley the future as hosted by Ato Molloka and "Sugar Corp," as we called the powerful government enterprise, beckoned from the lofty construction headquarters. Its perch offered a superb view of the caramel Omo bending away to the south into the basin under an arching sky fringed by high clouds. On the north side of the vast site the Omo flowed into the future plantation through a man-made lake that penned up the river briefly before channeling its waters into the main irrigation canal.

The placid scene masked the tensions crackling throughout the lands we surveyed. The month before, a construction truck had killed a young Bodi, setting off reprisals by other young men. Many of the Bodi, we learned, had never seen a truck. In dusk or darkness, headlights transformed the vehicles into mesmerizing, growling beasts. The lethality of these predators enraged the Bodi. Two project workers and two Government of Ethiopia security personnel had died in the counterattacks. Consultations among the government, Sugar Corp and the surrounding communities collapsed.

Ever ready to put a positive spin on troubling news, Molloka claimed relations had settled back into a peaceful rhythm only weeks later. Molloka said he had rushed back from a central committee meeting of the ruling party in Addis Ababa and convened elders to soothe the raw emotions. His security chief reported that community leaders had eased tensions by condemning revenge attacks and bringing the suspected perpetrators to the police.

Two dozen Bodi men who met with us three days later under a tree in a village, out of earshot of the local government man, offered a different account. The men passed snuff around in a spent bullet casing as they related how family members of young Bodi men suspected in the violence had handed them to authorities out of fear. The men described government coercion rather than the persuasion that Molloka touted, saying their planting land along the Omo already had been taken. They expressed worries about losing land, cattle and their culture to the sugar project. Do something about this, the men pleaded.

Back in Addis Ababa, the sugar daddies already had in mind a new diet and less exercise for Omo bovines, a rather less bucolic and free-ranging vision for pastoral life. At Sugar Corp headquarters, a senior official spoke of "zero grazing" as a desirable way to limit movement of cattle while fattening them on sugarcane waste. His deputy, who had accompanied us in South Omo, promptly seemed to contradict this line, insisting that grazing land was never touched. The senior official emphasized that the resettlement plan for pastoralists preceded the sugar plantation project as part of a government plan to "change their way of life."

Strangely however, sugar wasn't that big a deal in the Ethiopian way of life. While hawkers sold chunks of raw sugarcane on the streets for the casual gourmand, the Ethiopian appetite for sweets fell far behind the cravings of other imperial lands such as India, Turkey or Ethiopia's onetime nemesis, Italy. Pastry, candies and ice cream never enthralled the masses, in part because the country remained overwhelmingly rural and had limited contact with modern tastes.

Ethiopia's rapidly expanding beverage industry – carbonated drinks like Coca-Cola, whose bottles taught you the Amharic letter shaped like a shepherd's crook and pronounced "koh" – did signal the escalation of sugar demand as population and incomes grew. The main idea was that Ethiopia was just such a darn good place to grow sugarcane. The suitable soil, abundant water, and conducive climate meant that average sugarcane production per hectare, an area equal to 2.5 acres, is "very high compared to other countries," around nine to 11 tons versus six to eight tons elsewhere, according to an Ethiopian Investment Agency study.

The Dutch company HVA had developed a second sugarcane site, and the Ethiopians followed with a third at century's end. Omo Kuraz was by far the largest of three more sites under development. And yet the Ethiopians had identified seven other areas totaling 750,000 acres, twice the area of the Omo project, which could become sugar lands. Ethiopia's planners envisioned a bigger market than domestic sugar consumers: there was a whole world out there addicted to carbohydrates. While sugar meant more business for dentists and fitness trainers, the popularity of all things sugary reflected the rise in global prosperity after the collapse of the bitter Cold War in the 1990s. Freedom and sugar just went together.

About two-thirds of the world's sugar output comes from sugarcane grown in tropical or sub-tropical conditions. The rest comes from sugar beet harvested in more temperate climates. World demand grows about 1.4 percent a year, meaning that in the third decade of the 21st century, global production would need to increase by millions of tons to keep up. In a world market dominated by Brazil and India, yet constantly in need of more supply, Ethiopia spotted an opportunity to squeeze into the sugarcane sweepstakes.

The Bodi were rather central to the story here as they occupied lands adjacent to the massive Omo Kuraz footprint. Ato Molloka had persuaded some to move onto villagized footprints on the plantation site, becoming model tenants. We went to visit one settlement and were greeted by a grizzled old man domed by a cowboy hat – the Model Villager, we would later dub him over beers. Model Villager overflowed with excitement about his new habitat and the villagization experiment.

Yet within sight of the Omo, clean water turned out to be an issue. Sugar Corp sometimes locked the new borehole wells behind fences, forcing the aspiring model villagers to trek to the river itself for drinking water. If a waterborne illness lurked in that river, quenching your thirst might end up rather gut wrenching.

Infrastructure at the villagization sites rendered some areas barely habitable. At one, officials showed us a new cinder block school of eight classrooms, an administration building, and teachers' quarters. None was furnished or occupied. And although a visiting health worker was offering checkups, there was no clinic, suggesting he was brought in for show. The biggest problem was that irrigable land wasn't ready, meaning residents relied on food aid or trekked to their old lands for sustenance. Inside a warehouse, 200-pound sacks of grain were piled up, along with seed and machetes and water containers for household use. About 100 yards away stood a grain mill ready to receive maize from those new plots allocated to the villagized.

While land remained the prize in this epic tug of war, the government's plan drew some surprising support. Women residents – Bodi and the nearby Kwegu people who fished the river – expressed satisfaction with access to better drinking water and the prospect that their children would be educated. And Sugar Corp was training young people in carpentry, electrical work, and other skills in hopes of hiring some of them. Not everyone wanted to cling to the old, exhausting, male-centric ways.

Yet for these people, one impulse resonated, deeply rooted. Land is life. About 25 miles east in Hailewuha village, Mursi men and women, interviewed separately, spoke of similar concerns yet with far greater defiance than the Bodi.

"If he wants our land, first he has to come and destroy us, then he can take our land," said one man through a translator.

Villagers said they were waiting to see how the Bodi fared in the initial villagization push before considering the government's offer. The Mursi had reason to feel wary. Many recalled the government's resettlement of Konso farmers on Bodi grazing lands in 2006, an ill-considered episode of social shuffling that provoked violence. One man said the Mursi don't want to adopt the "highlander" approach of grazing cattle on small plots. Mursi women, famed for their protruding clay lip-plates, which many of them removed once the tourists and their handlers drove off, were more emphatic that the government wasn't to be trusted.

A woman whose lips now hung like rubbery hoops with the heavy clay disk absent pointed to nearby road building through the bush. That track appeared without Mursi permission, as evidence of the project's encroachment, she claimed. Another woman voiced what was on everyone's mind. "Is this peace development or war development?"

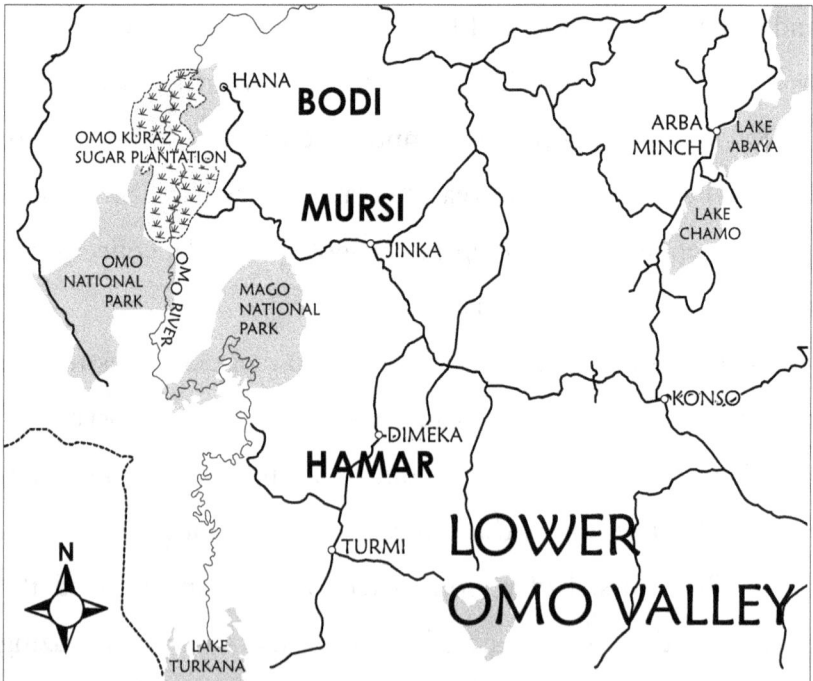

4

The Human Zoo

IN THE SLEEPY DOMESTIC-FLIGHTS wing at Addis Ababa airport, the departure lounge stirred to life with unseemly activity. Glancing up from a book, I took in a wide-angle view of the commotion.

The Ethiopian Airlines flight to Arba Minch in a 76-seat Bombardier Q400 turboprop usually drew a subdued two or three dozen Ethiopian students and merchants who plopped down in the hard plastic seats at the gate to await a shrill, hurried boarding call. Among the regulars would be grandmothers heading home from the big city, aid workers, missionaries, a handful of military personnel and maybe a few stubbornly independent tourists. Not so today. This flight would loft a pack of southbound irregulars.

American voices coarsened by tenacious winters shuffled into seats in front of me. Crisp khaki vests burst with pockets for stuffing film, notebooks and who knows what – the uniform of a 1970s white adventurer plunging into the African bush like a television god. Canons and Nikons armed with bulky telephoto lenses studded the throng. Stiff new baseball caps crowned graying noggins, emblazoned with the familiar yellow rectangle of a legendary international magazine.

For three weeks in Ethiopia, the retirees and near-retirees and the merely delusional had handed over 11,000 dollars each to the National Geographic Society, around 10 times more than the average Ethiopian would earn in a year. Next stop: the Valley of the Lower Omo.

As obnoxious and corrosive an act as raising a camera lens into the face of an imagined cultural primitive could be, the images did burst forth in pixels of wonderment. Photographing these people could be thrilling, a taste of the forbidden in a world rapidly morphing into a numbing uniformity of half-witted rumors and innuendos, oversexed entertainment, and Silicon Valley gadget porn.

Somehow these drive-by photographers fancied themselves as documenters of lost tribes. In fact, for the enterprises taking them into the Omo Valley and for the human exotica poised each day to be discovered, the visitors very much were the object of the show.

Yet there was a time when the Omo enigma did beckon fresh and intoxicating, and reasonably untouched. In the late 1960s and early 1970s, an intrepid band of anthropologists ventured into the Lower Omo Valley to document the mysterious Stone Age world of its inhabitants. Among those pioneers were Ivo Strecker, a dashing German, and his cheerful, sandy-haired British wife Jean Lydall, who met at the London School of Economics.

Anthropologists like Ivo and Jean bounced into Jinka, south of Arba Minch, in small planes that dropped them like commandos onto a grassy airstrip. I know this because one evening I stood high above Jinka, drink in hand, while an older Ivo pointed all this out as the descending orb crimsoned the sky.

A 1970 photograph taken in southern Ethiopia shows a smiling Jean, with pen poised over an open notebook, interviewing a middle-aged Hamar man wearing a chunky and quite stylish necklace over his bare chest. A thinner Ivo looks on while cradling his infant son between the legs of his khakis. Over their shoulders, two topless young Hamar women radiate smiles as they observe the fledgling researchers immersed in their world.

Ivo and Jean would focus their intellectual gifts on the Hamar for decades, producing studies, lectures, and documentary films to bring the Hamar worldview to the world in tumult beyond. In *The Perils of Face*, a volume of essays on southern Ethiopia cultures that Ivo inscribed to me: "Good journey!" Ivo tells of the most important part of the Hamar persona: *barjo*, a "concept of continuous creation" that any self-help guru at an incense-infused desert retreat would envy.

The gist is this. Every living being and even natural phenomena such as clouds and stars need barjo to achieve a state of order and well-being. Ivo explains that the Hamar distinguish between what someone is and what someone does. When disorder enters the picture, the deed draws condemnation rather than the doer. Loss of face, sin, and shame simply don't perturb this cosmos.

"What counts is the barjo of the people, that is, their well balanced and harmonic power to live," Ivo observes. "If your barjo is rich, you will act well. You will be socially competent and able to assert your own sphere of action as well as to respect the interests of others."

Barjo tended to wobble wherever anthropologists clustered in the Omo Valley in numbers alarming to Ato Molloka and his minions. One ritual gathering place stood out. Atop the hill from which we surveyed Jinka, with Molloka somewhere out there wrapping up his day of homage to the state, Ivo, Jean, and other scholars, with German funding, had built the South Omo Research Center.

The center was partly an ethnographic museum and gift shop with displays on the varied Omo peoples and their peculiar ways of doing things. One group poked through cow entrails to divine the meaning of events. The Hamar drew attention for their celebrated male initiation rite of "bull jumping" – naked young men scampering over the backs of several bulls, with sexual undertones involving their sisters.

The South Omo Research Center lorded over Jinka like a mountaintop palace, no doubt leaving Molloka steaming in his humble compound below. We wondered whether the howling sound system Ivo complained about from a church positioned nearby might be a counter-offensive in this culture war.

Displays in the museum revealed weapons, musical instruments, and ceremonial garments, some more earthy and less refined than others. In a building across the lawn, simple rooms waited for visiting scholars and observers. Barrels of rainwater served the bathrooms. For a few nights the research center became our base. And that meant dinner under the stars with Ivo and Jean.

As darkness snuggled the hilltop and the constellations swung onto the celestial stage, candles flickered in a soft breeze, casting a warm, cinematic glow across our table. Ivo sported a thick, graying beard, a youthful thatch of hair and dark, intense eyes. Woven tightly into his life's tapestry, the Omo Valley never wandered far from his thoughts. Jean spoke in measured, quiet bursts as if her thoughts were trying to find words supple enough to convey the layers of meaning she had seen and heard during encounters with the Hamar. She would pause, tweak her sentence, nod and carry on.

As the conversation unfurled, we passed around a simple fare of stews and nacho chips washed down by wine. The main course, of course, was the tales these two told of watching the Omo Valley transformed. Ivo and Jean could remember a time when these lands teemed with big wildlife – giraffe, buffalo, and lion. A Hamar man who slayed a big cat earned great honor for the rest of his life. Such opportunities for glory must be exceptionally rare today after civil war, population growth, and road building intruded. Lions seemed to lounge elsewhere.

Not all had passed into memory, however. Hamar women still strolled around bare-breasted, their hair cut short in braided dreadlocks and dyed in the reddish pigment that gave them all an almost sci-fi look, like an ancient, galactic band of automatons.

It was the men in this culture who stood out, who took pride in prettying themselves to attract the ladies. A thick dollop of reddish clay crowned their heads, with a fuzzy ball attached to the forehead and a feather dancing from the back of the cranium. What could one say? These guys looked like chickens.

Jean had succeeded spectacularly over the years in bringing Hamar culture to mass audiences in the muddled "modern" world. She shunned "voice of God" external commentary as imposing distance with the peoples she documented. Her films let the Hamar talk, with questions coming from off camera. The 1990 film *The Women Who Smile* introduces the not-yet-married and still carefree Duka. A glint of rebellion mixes with resignation in Duka's eyes as she spies her freedom slipping away with the approach of marriage. Duka takes a break from the sorghum harvest on the land left by her deceased mother and fields questions from Jean about the harsh gender roles of Hamar culture.

"Why wasn't I a boy? I say when my hands ache from grinding" grain, Duka laments.

Jean turns to Bonko, a young man helping with the harvest, to probe the gender chasm.

From off-camera: "Bonko, wouldn't you like to be a woman? Isn't it good to be a woman?" (Duka and her female friend break out in laughter.)

Bonko, chuckling as he snaps his hand through the air: "A woman's beaten. A man isn't. At the dance she's beaten. When she marries, she's beaten."

Off camera: "Will you beat your wife?"

Bonko: "I will beat her! It's the custom. If you don't beat her, she won't listen. She'll wander off in the lowlands."

In a fascinating paper for the International Conference of Ethiopian Studies, Jean delves into beating rituals and how they form an integral part of male-female relationships and male initiation ceremonies. The whippings are carried out with a long, thin, and flexible tree branch stripped of leaves. The whips are not always wielded in anger or for punishment. At dances with boys and men, threatened or actual whippings might signal that a girl's flirtation has gained attention, according to Jean.

"A girl who gets whipped will feel she has made an amorous conquest, and will happily sport the scars which prove it, not unlike the city girl who sports a silver bracelet to prove she has an admirer," Jean writes. Duka agrees that girls like this behavior.

"'Yes, because we are young," Jean quotes Duka as explaining. "'Being young we seek to be beaten. When you are young you want to experience everything.'"

Jean's film series became so famous that the legendary Hollywood industry newspaper Variety reviewed a sequel on Duka, called *Duka's Dilemma*, declaring that it "offers spicy promise of soap-opera situations and exotic rituals." Eight years on, Duka's husband Sago has taken a second wife, and emotional fireworks ensue. As reality television was dawning in America, Variety gushed: "The resulting, sometimes fascinating plunge into domestic drama would feel voyeuristic if subjects did not clearly welcome Lydall's camera as witness, confidant and sounding-board."

Broadcast on television and shown at festivals and symposiums, Jean's films achieved an astonishing level of intimacy that she acknowledged made some people uncomfortable. In an interview with a German institute, Jean pointed to an outdoor childbirth scene in *Duka's Dilemma* in which the attending women pour water over a bewildered newborn girl and then scrape her skin, commenting on what they think are signs of an infection. Sorry, kid. The Hamar welcome to just-arrived entrants in the human race is a bracing contrast to the soft-focus reverie of an American birth scene. Before broadcasting the film, Jean previewed it in the Hamar birth village. "Is this OK to show to strangers?" Yes, they said, it's nice.

The Omo world into which that girl was born would look far different from what her grandmother had experienced during a lifetime. A European Union study that examined both South Omo Zone and the Turkana region just over the border in Kenya – essentially one thirsty pastoral ecosystem – ticked off the issues. Any one of these would be a game changer; taken together they threatened to rewrite the destiny of these lands and peoples.

"The main sources of vulnerability in the border areas are (1) periodic and unpredictable resource scarcity and recurrent disasters (droughts, epizootics, etc.); (2) mounting pressure on critical resources, especially land and water, by (a) land alienation to agro-industry schemes, (b) rapid population growth and (c) climate change and ecosystem degradation."

Imagine what the Hamar, unaccustomed to fancy terms like "epizootics" and "land alienation" must feel while hearing this list of woe. This is going to do wonders for our barjo.

These pressures were more than a century in the making. After Emperor Menelik II's soldiers famously repulsed an Italian invasion through the tricky passes of mountainous Adwa on the empire's northern frontier in March 1896, turning Menelik into a global celebrity, a liberating chapter opened for the highlanders. Ancient Ethiopia would avoid the fate of much of Africa, carved up by Europeans into spheres of influence, economic plunder, and stiff servitude. Menelik seized on the victory and his fame to propel Ethiopia into the modern world. Resplendent in a royal headdress, bedazzling cape, and ivory tunic for photographers, he was thoroughly modern off camera.

Menelik introduced automobiles, electricity, and telephones to the burgeoning imperial capital below the Entoto Hills and opened the first bank and modern schools. In 1904, the emperor welcomed a contingent of United States Marines sent by President Teddy Roosevelt to formally initiate diplomatic and trade relations. America's allure as a frontier market seems to have captured the monarch's imagination: a Belgian explorer just back from "Abyssinia" told the New York Times in 1909 that Menelik was heavily invested in American railroad stocks.

The fierce defender of Ethiopia from European encroachment lived until 12 December 1913 – ironically, 50 years to the day before neighboring Kenya slipped the grasp of the British Empire and began its journey as an independent state.

Yet Ethiopian independence, while far ahead of the African curve, remained a delicate creation. Like the longevity of bright yellow Meskel flowers that carpet the terrain of northern Ethiopia every year, a change of political seasons would sweep away both beauty and freedom. Four decades after the victory at Adwa the Italians returned, this time with thundering bombers and terrifying nerve gas, and fearsome mechanized infantry propelled by ruthless commanders. Mussolini's forces overran the disorganized, lightly armed defenses of the imperial realm then under Emperor Haile Selassie's rule, horrifying people the world over in the 1930s.

In the late 1800s, Menelik had taken a page from the European aggressors' playbook and pushed south from the highlands of Amhara toward the pastoralist lowlands abutting today's Sudan and Kenya. This area constituted a transition zone, where people and their herds moved across an immense terrain of grass and shrub, studded here and there with spindly termite mounds. Mountain ranges rose dramatically across the topography and bifurcated grasslands into basins. Through one of these basins threaded the Omo River itself.

The military victories of the highland armies, which often led to enslavement of the conquered, rocked the social order of the Indigenous peoples in the lowlands. Some, like the Hor, also known as the Arbore, built a new narrative as a kind of cultural survival mechanism, as the Japanese sociologist Yukio Miyawaki discovered through his research.

"Hor despise Amhara rule and have tried to eliminate its influence from their lives," he wrote in *The Perils of Face*. "But the memory of the Amhara conquest has been incorporated into their patriarchal ideology, and paradoxically, their cultural identity has been constructed on the basis of this memory."

Miyawaki documented stories passed down by the Hor people that connect their political downfall to highlander power with the decline of local chieftains and their spirit powers. Their authority wanes after a confrontation with a gun-toting explorer, apparently the American doctor Arthur Donaldson Smith, one of the first whites to come through the area, in the 1890s. The lore of Hor says that guardian spirits disappear, a sign of the impending dispersion of their peoples. Yet the Hor bounce back over the coming decades and wily leaders emerge in the mid-20th century to channel Ethiopian authority into their own power base.

Something quite similar happens in Molloka's ancestral neighborhood. Over the Maale people ruled a divine king with chiefdoms below him. Tribute in the form of elephant ivory and leopard skins marked high status. To triumph in a brave hunt against wild animals conferred prestige in life and in death. Special songs would serenade a great hunter at his funeral.

The rise of Menelik as the unifying leader of Ethiopia's fiefdoms, the king of kings, spread Ethiopian highland power far to the south. Menelik's underlings, like those of Meles a century later, pushed into Maale lands and set up garrisons on high points. The Maale persuaded Menelik to stop seizing their children as slaves.

Gradually Ethiopian power grew deeper roots as the locals themselves nurtured the new political reality. In the 1960s, Protestant missionaries further opened the Maale people to a new system of belief and outsider ideas of the possible. After 1963, as the era of African independence took hold, so too did a dramatic transformation of the Maale political-economic culture. The Maale elite had become, in the words of anthropologist Donald Donham, "Ethiopian landlords." Rites of divine kingship and control over trade mattered less than assimilation to the highlander Ethiopian culture: "the ability to use and to influence the Ethiopian state apparatus, and above all the ownership of land – an institution backed and regulated by the power of the Ethiopian state."

The new Maale king Bailo bought a house in Jinka and enrolled his sons in school there. Scandalously, he removed his regal necklace when going into town. "In Maale, the necklace was the most sacred insignia of kingship; in town, it merely identified Bailo as pagan and provincial," Donham explains in his book, *Work and Power in Maale, Ethiopia.* "Henceforth he would live as an 'Amhara' he proclaimed; he would not observe old Maale taboos."

Three decades later, Molloka inherited this legacy as a high school student. Because a conflict between the Maale and Bana peoples had broken out, going to school in Jinka proved too dangerous; students were being killed on the way. At his parents' insistence, he returned to his village to herd cattle. One day the Ethiopian People's Revolutionary Democratic Front, the ethnic federalist political coalition of the new Ethiopia led by Meles, showed up looking for someone who could translate from Amharic to the Maale language.

Molloka's work as a translator led to his assignment to the peace committee of the kebele, the first step of his climb up the ladder of Ethiopian power.

By and large, the Hamar refused to mingle so intimately with highlander power. Once a Hamar, always a Hamar. A shaman in a village about 15 miles from the border with Kenya personified the Hamar commitment to tradition and insistence on holding their cultural ground. The old man sat, speaking in a soft, slightly hoarse voice. His skin the color of dark coffee, ritually scarred on his chest in a pattern of furrowed dashes. His head depicted elegance in the Hamar style. Above high cheekbones, clay arranged in orange and white strips arced across the forefront of his skull. A band of wiry gray hair ran behind, after which reddish-orange clay in a grid pattern brought up the rear.

The shaman had extended calming moral support to an outsider who had come to help these people grasp at useful strands of the modern world. He assured the outsider that her efforts could make headway, and indeed he was right. Modest assistance had energized strong, resourceful women in Hamar villages. They learned basic Amharic, numeracy, and personal hygiene, and formed a community-managed trading center. These Hamar females would cling to the ways that bound them one to another, while gaining a tantalizing glimpse of that outside universe threatening to upset their barjo.

The Hamar had some sense of their landscape being squeezed by the government's plans. Three men sat under a tree late one August afternoon, atop a hill 5 degrees north of the Equator whose panorama took in a sweeping plain below edged by distant mountains. Sheep milled around in a soft breeze near scattered tukuls – Ethiopia's classic mud-walled circular huts topped by thatch roofs.

"Our fear is that we will be put on a small amount of land near the Nyangatom," a people across the Omo River to the west, one of the men explained alongside short green tendrils poking through the hilltop dirt. "We are all fighting for the same grassland, grass for cattle. The Arbore farm near the river, and we are like family. But with the Nyangatom, the Dassanech, and the Borena, we fight."

The human-zoo tourists and their camera lenses tended to treat the Omo peoples as noble savages without grasping the complexity of their cultures and their ordeal of survival. Look at that boy scamper nekkid across them bulls. Click. That Hamar chick is kinda cute. Click. Check out that crazy lip-stretching clay plate. Click. (I bought one of these Mursi lip disks and was astonished at its weight; no wonder women removed them as soon as the tourists left the village.)

One woman with a grounded grasp of what the Mursi faced in this drama of land and water had come all the way from Canada to dish Omo dirt. Shauna LaTosky studied Mursi women and their modern dilemmas and served as director of the South Omo Research Center. That made her a lightning rod for the government's disdain. It didn't help that Shauna toiled for what the Ethiopian overlords must have viewed as a diabolical foreign snooping operation – Germany's eminent Max Planck Institute for Social Anthropology, where she had the temerity to work as a post-doctoral researcher in the Department of Integration and Conflict.

After a decade of research among the Mursi, Shauna published *Predicaments of Mursi (Mun) Women in Ethiopia's Changing World.* Her book described how these women use rhetoric, from oratory to body movements, and even "the role of silence," as one reviewer noted, to carve out influence in a patriarchal society. In a related academic paper, Shauna complained that images of the Mursi proliferating in coffee-table books, travel blogs, and online photographs meant to display them as exotic primitives were utterly disconnected from the current reality of these girls and women. Shauna wrote that for decades Ethiopia's highlander government administrators had seized on these "exotic representations" of the Mursi as evidence of their need for civilizing.

The Mursi cultural object and practice that attracts camera-toting tourists while repelling gender-rights activists is the famed stretched-lip plate. Mursi men and women admire the beauty and "virtues of strength and competence" conveyed by the lip-plate, according to Shauna. "One of the practical implications of this paper thus lies in my suggestion to look more carefully at the mechanisms by which the Ethiopian state, non-state organizations, and individuals impose their will on the bodies of

Ivo Strecker (left) and Shauna LaTosky (center) at the South Omo Research Center

Mursi women and how Mursi women are experiencing and, in some cases, resisting such impositions."

When talking about the Mursi, Molloka would get quite worked up. He raised his voice and his gaze hardened. He fingered two culprits in the Mursi's resistance to government plans: a handful of Mursi activists who had taken to the Internet to draw attention and NGOs – "nongovernmental organizations" – and tourists with a salvation-preservation streak.

"They want the Mursi to be a museum, to take photographs and videos," Molloka observed. "So when we talk about bringing services, they are opposed, because the Mursi will be changed and can't be photographed as they were."

Molloka seemed genuinely disgusted by foreign tourists coming down to gawk at Omo villagers. The solution, he explained to us, was to take control of the business. Henceforth there would be a museum of South Omo peoples and cultural village sites where visitors could witness rituals in a dignified setting. In other words, he seemed to be suggesting: if we're going to have a human zoo, I'm going to be the zookeeper.

5

Molloka No Mursi

THE RAINS PICKED UP in Addis Ababa, and residents scurried about, fleece jackets cinched against the damp, chilling winds raking the high-altitude Ethiopian capital. August drenched the soul in highland Ethiopia, smothered your mood in a blanket of gray, swirling mist and ethereal thunder, and sent you splashing across muddied streets and concrete streams toward steaming cups of macchiato.

If you couldn't get out of the country, then escaping the Addis maelstrom would suffice. Dry and warmer conditions beckoned in the southern lowlands almost 650 miles closer to the Equator. The change in meteorology would lift our spirits and make journeys along sandy roads an easy task. This time the dusty Stone Age looked like a welcome retreat from the dripping New Flower.

Almost a year after Meles the Great Leader's passing, and

nine months since my first visit, Ethiopia's international partner governments readied once more to head into the mysterious Valley of the Lower Omo. This time we plotted a more ambitious journey, first visiting with the cow blood-sipping Mursi, the people most resistant to Molloka's designs, and also spending time with the more pliable Bodi. Then we would venture southward to the celebrated Hamar and related Tsemay peoples close to the Kenya border.

Our team would rumble into action again under the auspices of the DAG, the multi-government Development Assistance Group, influential forum for all of Ethiopia's international funders, the United States included – in cash, credit, or conundrum. The task set for us: size up how well the villagization push was going and look for signs of hostile intent – or outright hostilities – from the federal democratic republic.

Joining Peter and I on this trip was Patrick, a slender German diplomat in his 30s who quickly adopted the spirit of our group. Patrick punctuated his pensive, official demeanor with outbursts of laughter at the absurdities the Omo Valley tossed our way. Together we would venture through the Omo Kuraz plantation in the far west to see whether sugarcane and villagization really were taking hold and somehow yoked in harmony along the vast irrigation channels emerging along the Omo River.

As the international activists claimed, were the pastoralists truly being rounded up, or worse, and forced off their ancient grazing lands? What kinds of pressure were they facing from the sugar juggernaut? Could the Indigenous peoples somehow adapt and hang on, clinging to their body art, bracelets, and bare skin? What should be our message to the revolutionary anti-democrats back in the capital?

These concerns, plus the considerable logistics for the journey and contacts with the government, consumed the attention of our beaming trip leader, Melanie, whom I guessed to be in her late 30s. Melanie traded a comfy office in the sprawling British Embassy compound in Addis Ababa with its forest, horse stables, and six-hole golf course, for the bumpy back seat of a Land Rover.

Melanie would add considerable heft to our expedition, for she ran Britain's development affairs in Ethiopia, and Ethiopia was Britain's biggest destination for development aid – and a troublesome one at that. It wasn't just the Ethiopian Spice Girls stirring up trouble. The clever and kinetic British-funded pop music group Yegna, an unorthodox development creation designed to reflect, and inspire, archetypes of female Ethiopian adolescence – from diva to humble village girl – had begun to draw the scorn of tabloids and politicians in London. Why was Britain spending millions on shaking up the playlists and video charts in faraway Ethiopia?

America tended to post highly capable journeypersons to run its development work in Ethiopia, leaving politics to the front office, meaning the ambassador's suite upstairs. Our witty and sociable chief Dennis, a quick study on inscrutable human rights issues, hailed from Illinois with expertise in agriculture. Dennis managed one of America's most complex foreign-aid portfolios, up to a billion dollars invested each year in 100 programs ranging from transforming health care and preventing AIDS to shrinking hunger, expanding literacy, bolstering civil rights, and spreading a social safety net for the poorest Ethiopians.

In Melanie the United Kingdom had dispatched an insider steeped in politics and sensitivity toward British prestige. Earlier, as principal private secretary to the secretary of state for the Department for International Development, usually called "DFID," Melanie had acquired a global perspective on British doings. Melanie now found herself in the bullseye of Parliament members and activists suspicious that British money was forcing dirt-poor, marginalized Africans off their communal lands. The British government was defending a human-rights lawsuit against its investment in Ethiopian government social services in a neighboring region, had lawyered up and grown nervous about the treatment of vulnerable pastoralists.

With an Oxford degree in modern history and another in development studies, Melanie toted admirable credentials into the Lower Omo Valley. Now she would kick the earth in South Omo and encounter Ethiopia at its most clever. Melanie, meet the Right Honourable Member of Paternalism, Ato Molloka.

Once again far-seeing America dispatched me into humanity's

homeland – a former international editor in Washington transformed into a dirt-kicking ethnologist and human rights monitor. America, I accept. Along with hiking boots, sunglasses, and durable nylon safari pants, I tossed emergency rations into my bag. Thanks to a small American military presence in Ethiopia, I had secured a cherished stash of Meals Ready to Eat – universally proclaimed MREs – and kept them under my desk. If we found ourselves far from reliable eateries, a river to fish, or a missionary's kitchen, I could simply rip open a putty-colored plastic MRE pouch, add water to the heating sleeve to set off a chemical reaction, and voila, a stunningly hot meal would appear.

Among the main courses offered by the manufacturer, three had become tolerable favorites: spaghetti with beef, chicken with noodles, and beef taco – every offering "War Fighter Tested – War Fighter Approved." America exploded from the pouch in a passel of condiments and junk food samples – the dollhouse-size Tabasco hot sauce bottle stood out – that delighted my European travel companions.

Just one other bit of unfinished business weighed on us. The number of humans who could speak and understand both English and the Mursi language probably could be counted on two hands, if that. The number of such humans that Molloka didn't know: in theory, zero. Ethiopia, ever suspicious, kept an eye on just about everyone who could represent a threat to the ruling party and the state's grand strategies. Molloka understandably made it his business to know what was going on across South Omo, across mountains, grasslands, streams, forests, and tribal tongues. Even across minds, it seemed. How could we find someone both capable and uncompromised by government meddling?

From a Christian charity, we learned of four Mursi young men going to school in Arba Minch, practically the other side of the moon for a Mursi villager and likely off the government's surveillance radar. The boys knew enough English to handle our conversations. We signed them up for what would be windfall wages back in the village.

On the first day of August, our convoy pulled into the South Omo Zone compound in Jinka. Ato Molloka took his seat at the top of the T, exquisitely well prepared. According to Molloka's account, he had turned into a veritable community activist since our last visit, touring woredas in his dominion to hear concerns directly from the people. Molloka boasted of pushing community consultations to "grassroots" levels. We wondered just how much dissent Ato Molloka could tolerate. At these meetings, what do you give as the goal of villagization – and do you describe alternatives? Melanie asked, almost teasing, I thought.

Ato Molloka spoke of his "experience sharing" program, taking Bodi and Mursi skeptics on the road, or goat path, to see up close how the government's plan to shift them toward farming was taking root. "We took them to the Dassanech and they saw that real pastoralists have irrigation farming," Molloka asserted, flinging out his hands for emphasis as if shaking water from his digits.

The Dassanech lived on parched lands right along the Kenya-Ethiopia border with a tantalizing view of distant Lake Turkana, the world's largest permanent desert lake. The same lake received the Omo waters that exited the sugar plantation. Within a year three-quarters of the Dassanech people would need emergency food aid to survive, as a powerful drought gripped Ethiopia.

Those who were convinced during these visits got irrigable plots of land back on home turf, while the holdouts asked why they got none, Molloka related. We asked about their free-ranging cattle. Have you given pastoral communities written agreements that they will retain access to their grazing lands if they villagize? Molloka bobbed and weaved, to borrow a term from an American college football announcer who was thinking boxing while watching a running back thread through defenses.

We need no agreement because the right of access is enshrined in the Ethiopian Constitution, Molloka retorted. Having no handy copy of this legal charter, we took his word. What's more, Molloka reported, both he and the Ethiopian Minister of Federal Affairs had given verbal assurances to the Bodi that their grazing would live on, a herbivore's ceaseless feast.

Molloka acknowledged that the government had done a poor job of providing seeds, tools, and farm training to the pastoralists and thus was making amends. "Pastoral associations" would be set up in resettlement villages to open the way to loans and market access. Parks and forests would be protected. Our Indigenous culture is our wealth, Molloka proclaimed, softening us up further. For instance, we will preserve places where the tribes conduct cultural ceremonies.

I had seen one of these intriguing areas marked on a map drawn up by a French staffer for the European Union who doubled as an amateur Omo anthropologist. On the rough diagram he had marked, "Mursi Secret Places." My imagination wandered back to the Hardy Boys mysteries of my youth, searchlights cutting through the foggy dark, clandestine caves, shadowy villains, totems, and treasure.

The Mursi not only carefully demarcated and protected sacred forest spaces known as *baa barrara*, but they also rather meticulously managed grazing and cultivation areas. These were no aimless wanderers chasing the next sunset. "Pastoralists Do Plan!" exulted the Mursi activist and researcher Olisarali Olibui and the Canadian anthropologist Shauna in an international newsletter on rangelands.

A central figure in the Mursi approach to sustainable land governance is known as the *komoru*. "The komoru together with Mursi elders can formally decide to ban the use of a watering point or grazing area," Olisarali and Shauna explain. "If the komoru makes such a decision, nobody will move to that area or interfere with his decision. He might also decide that a certain area should not be burned or order that the cattle have to go and live in a particular area."

However, the komoru doesn't only act as an arbiter of the common good, like a retired judge handling a property dispute in an American town before heading out to his tee time and bourbon at the golf club. This being Omo-land, an aspect of the divine infuses the komoru's obligations to land, people, and cattle.

"When the cattle have disease or are moved to a new place, the komoru must first carry out a ritual called *biyo lama* (blessing the cattle) and *rossen uro ma* (milking by the river)," the researchers explain. "When the cattle graze and drink in that place, the cattle will be healthy."

As our conversation with Molloka wound down, we brought out our aspiring translators. We wanted somehow to assure Molloka and his lieutenants that our youthful assistants carried no political grudges to the table, only linguistic longings. An activist-filmmaker we had used the previous year for translations had run afoul of Molloka. Our boys would talk a neutral line; stitching together the meaning of what we were hearing would be their sole interest. In retrospect, the boys needed to grasp only one meaning in this pitiful trade in tongues: we were hopelessly naïve.

The next morning our vehicles descended the sun-kissed escarpment west of Jinka and began our trek across the Omo Valley through Mago National Park. Our translators had walked

12 miles from their village to meet us. As emissaries to the world beyond the Omo Valley, they carried a considerable cultural burden across an unimaginable chasm. Their styles reflected this fused worldview. One boy wore a modern shirt complemented by a lion's tooth strung around his neck from a big cat he said he had felled.

Within three hours we had passed through Hana and reached the sprawling Omo Kuraz plantation site with its epic panorama. No longer a lowly, yawning ditch, the main irrigation canal carried diverted Omo for big-scale agriculture. Dense stands of sugarcane almost 10 feet high had cropped up. An initial 3,000 acres of sugarcane now occupied the banks of the Omo in phase one of the massive development. Ethiopia's dream indeed had taken shape. I turned to Nureddin, the Ethiopian project manager, who resembled the American comic actor Bill Murray. "You're really serious about this, aren't you?"

Elsewhere on the Omo Kuraz site, sugar refineries were being built to transform the cane into the commodity. A shanty town had sprung up a few miles north of the emerging fields around what appeared to be warehouses and housing for workers. Bodi men wearing togas and carrying staffs strolled past small shops with grass-weave walls. However, we soon learned that the experiment to create villages where Bodi herders would settle and farm on plots of land adjacent to the sugar fields seemed less cultivated than the cane.

"The government made me come first," said a sorghum farmer near the irrigation channel. He wore a white floppy hat and a dingy housecoat, leaving his leathered feet exposed in sandals. "The government chose some people, and I am one of them."

Upon further questioning, the farmer said he was commuting from his home village to the villagization site. For a society-shifting initiative, this sounded a bit tenuous. And suburban. Other farmers said they were lured to plots near the canal by government promises of good land for maize and sorghum. Maybe so, they said, yet without access to water, that was hard to judge. The sugar imbibed water aplenty, yet the villagized claimed only a trickle from the river.

The villages themselves held more promise and satisfied customers. About 3 o'clock in the afternoon, around 60 women and children gathered under a tree at a new village known as Belalong. The older women had shaved heads, ear lobes pierced and stretched and around 20 metallic bracelets that chimed as they clapped to make points. Approaching visitors with outstretched hands and bare breasts, the women greeted us with a hearty "Ay-bush-ee" in Bodi-speak. Tukul huts sprouted on a gentle hillside with broad views of the Omo basin.

At the nearby villagization site called Elogobia, we saw progress. Four water spigots were in place. About 500 yards away a school was operating grades one through four with learning

A Mursi man at work in his Omo Valley village

diagrams painted on the outside walls: math functions, parts of flowering plants, the Amharic and English alphabets, and images of the towering royal stelae still standing in the remains of Ethiopia's ancient imperial capital, Aksum, almost a thousand miles to the north.

Ethiopia's villagization plans exploited a gender divide. The men might grumble about grazing lands and farming potential, yet the women we talked with generally were fans of the water points and schools set up in the new villages. A water source close to a school near your hut meant the women would have a lot more time available to spend with their children, and with other women. This represented a heady dose of empowerment in male-dominated societies, a benefit that faraway activists often overlooked.

During our otherwise insightful field visit, a discordant note emerged. Ato Molloka had accompanied us west and took issue with the boys' translation of a Bodi focus group, which he said suggested that the agricultural Konso people were grabbing vacated Bodi land. In village parleys or Internet chatter, Molloka placed great value on the words used to describe how the government dealt with the delicate Omo.

That night as we relaxed back in Jinka at a local watering hole after our long day, the unofficial leader among our translators approached us timidly in the red cycling jersey he wore each day. "I don't feel well," he said. It wasn't cow's blood that he couldn't digest. The long arm of the Ethiopian state had turned his stomach, according to his telling. The previous evening, only hours after we had introduced them to Molloka and his team, the boys were visited at their hotel by two men who said they worked for the zonal administration. Don't cast the sugar project in a bad light through your translations, the men warned. These are foreigners that you're working for. You're Ethiopian. Ethiopia depends on their money.

What to do? From a lodge outside Jinka, Melanie worked the phones to government ministers back in Addis, reminding them of their assurances that we could do our research without interference. Clearly, however, it would be foolish and perhaps dangerous to venture into Mursi territory with these boys, putting them and their families at risk of reprisals from the omnipotent government. At 10:20 the next morning we returned to Molloka's office for a showdown – and a getaway.

Peter and I strolled into Molloka's chamber, along with Melanie and Patrick. We were all doing our best to look pissed. Melanie got down to business. We're disappointed. Our translators are being intimidated and might be harmed. This has undermined our ability to conduct our research. "It's very important to us that they be left free" without any government officials threatening their safety. "This is your zone, and we ask that you take responsibility," Melanie said firmly.

Around the table we went, heaping on the disappointment. "We started two days ago with promises of openness and access," I reminded Molloka. "Our goal was a larger view of the situation."

Ato Molloka bobbed. And weaved. In my zone nobody will intimidate anyone, and if it happens, that person will be held responsible. Let me look into it. We're happy that you hired student translators without a political bent. He suggested that the boys could drop by his office to receive his personal assurance of satisfaction. Like that was going to happen.

I felt the sensation of our entourage being expelled from this part of Omo country. Our plans had gone seriously awry, and it was time for quick pivot, a dose of adaptation. In the Omo Valley, improvisation came in handy. Improv among humans here was about as common as the double-helix twisted in new directions by natural selection – shaped by climate, random changes in flora and fauna, or the Darwinian priorities of powerful outsiders.

Having made clear that we would hold Molloka to account for the boys' safety and would get them back to their village, we turned our sights to the south, to Hamar country. We're headed next to Turmi, in Hamar Woreda, and we want you to keep away from our translators there, we told Molloka. We'll come back to the Mursi another time. The Hamar anchored the southern stretches of South Omo Zone, far from the sprawling sugar plantation, and their experience would instruct us on the positives and pitfalls of the government's social engineering of the Omo Valley. Probed in books and films, the Hamar also stood out as the most famous of the Omo cultures.

Shedding our frustration with missing the Mursi, we felt our anticipation growing as we departed. Our convoy sped from Ato Molloka's compound, drove out past the anthropologists' old airstrip and pointed toward the dusty skies leading toward Kenya.

6

Develop Us Silly

TWO PALE-SKINNED MEN are lugging backpacks through an idyllic, savagely green rainforest, pondering their mission into a strange and puzzling land. As they descend on a cluster of thatch-roofed huts under a lush canopy of soaring trees, one of the men reveals their mission: to understand how to help the inhabitants of this bewildering jungle rise from their elemental existence.

As the oddball outsiders wander their surroundings in ties and dress shirts, making notes on a clipboard, they sense that something is awry. Our intrepid experts observe half-naked forest dwellers harvesting a bounty from the river, fish joyfully leaping into their net. Not far away, a man whose hair shoots out in looping tendrils strolls by smiling, with recently caught forest critters dangling cheerfully from a pole. The scene shifts to children sprawled on the ground, grinning with delight as an elder in a towering headdress regales them with stories. Well, this is awkward. These people already seem enchanted by life, sustainably so.

"So all we could really bring them," the men conclude, stroking their briefcases and exchanging furtive glances, "was development."

The experts feel obliged to explain to the natives what's wrong with paradise. Villagers are baffled by a byzantine flowchart linking "threats" to "strengths" and "opportunities." Some residents lounge in the dirt, daydreaming, or play with their kids, refusing to join in "participatory community project building." Efforts to get the forest folks fired up about "income generating activities" also falter because they're quite satisfied with living on less than a dollar a day. And, by the way, what's a dollar?

Undaunted, the giddy interlopers dig deeper into their briefcases and summon reinforcements. "Stakeholders" arrive to unleash public-private partnerships, sending a road-building bulldozer slashing through pristine terrain. The locals gaze bewildered at an electrified fence girdling their treasured forest just as a colorful bird alights on the crackling barbed wire and tumbles lifeless to the ground.

Inevitably the traumatized villagers are reduced to a sliver of land in a gray, apocalyptic urbanscape with cars whizzing by. Flanked by bug-eyed former villagers, the beaming development men bask in victory. "Welcome to the global village," they gush.

Created by writer and illustrator Oren Ginzburg for Survival International, the animated short "There You Go!" became an instant hit within the democracy and governance team, stealth entertainment, just as soon as the tale dropped into our inboxes at the American Embassy. In one simple parable Ginzburg skewered the touchstones of our trade, delighting Carol the office chief. She joked that the video's main characters resembled me and our bearded conflict-mitigation adviser with an amiable drawl from the wilds of southern Virginia and an encyclopedic knowledge of southern Ethiopia. We have come with the gift of development. We understand that you may choose to decline our gracious offer and run for your lives.

The video was no mere satirical gem. Survival International used the fable to solicit donations from irate Westerners spurred to hyper indignation by the cartoon misadventures of white men running wild in the African forest. "The government of Ethiopia, which is one of the biggest recipients of American and British overseas aid, is forcibly resettling 200,000 self-sufficient tribal people, including Mursi, Kwegu and Bodi, leaving thousands with no land, cattle herds or livelihood," the organization asserted on its web site. Donations poured in as did furious e-mails, choking Dennis's inbox, as the chief American development official in Ethiopia.

As a juicy target for international ire, the Omo lands captured several repugnant themes at once. Big agriculture crushes noble savages. Rapacious modernity attacks the vestiges of ancient African culture. Greedy authoritarian government oppresses peace-loving peoples of Mother Earth. The activists' campaigns drew a stark contrast. Yet in the Omo we found gradations that challenged these narratives. Some of the Hamar welcomed the chance to tap into irrigation farming as drought settled over their traditional lands, a likely effect of the world's overheating climate engine. Maybe some reliable health care would be indigenously delightful too.

Only education could be a sensitive offering, freighted with highlander values and implications of state power over Hamar children. Impressionable minds might well be worth fighting for, mind you. Even so, Hamar land seemed less tense than Mursi territory.

Peter, ever thoughtful about what we were seeing on the ground as the representative for Irish Aid, would observe that development was transitioning from something that "happens" to people in a needy land to a set of choices in which they should have a say. In Ethiopia, Ireland promoted the virtues of citizen involvement anchored in human rights and government accountability, its influence among the donor governments far more pronounced than you would expect from such a small nation. Ethiopia listened to Ireland.

To extract answers from the Omo peoples, we carried with us to all village visits a questionnaire blessed by the Development

Assistance Group, which sounds like the kind of faceless outfit that might have sent Ginzburg's characters on their rollicking mission to freak out forest dwellers. We came with clipboards too and a determination to fill all those blanks with meaning.

Getting through the questions could prove tedious for a subsistence farmer or herder who had chores on his mind, rituals to obey, and limited contact with faraway notions of formal education. Sitting on a log for an hour or two, while swatting away flies and our insistent queries, did not exactly summon communal bliss.

One small matter deserved delicate handling. We had to explain carefully that we would be sucking information from them and not paying for it. Villagers had grown used to human-zoo tourists showing up, and they received payments from tourism companies for the privilege of helping the drop-in visitors get up close and personal with earth-intoxicated sapiens. An Ethiopian fixer usually went ahead of us to explain all this to the village elders; once the French armchair anthropologist did us a massive favor by spending a week moving among villages to prep elders. We're researchers, not tourists, and would you care for the Beaujolais or the chardonnay?

We gathered under trees, rarely inside any structure. Sometimes we sat in the sand for a distinctly ground-level view. A flat rock might cushion our rear ends. Maybe the locals would bring out traditional wooden stools for us. While we received these courtesies with gratitude, squatting on paleo furnishings made one pine for a comfy leather sofa.

Women usually were interviewed separately because outsiders would hear little from them in a mixed group. Gender norms gave men the preeminent and pretty much only voice. Children tended to orbit our gatherings, leaving a trail of giggles, especially when we turned our smiles in their direction. Goats, chickens, dogs, lizards, and cows all might grace us with appearances, sometimes chattering away, sometimes gliding past lost in other thoughts of the day. Unfortunately for biodiversity and ecosystem inclusivity, we solicited views solely from the top of the food chain.

On my first visit to the valley, Paul, Peter, Emma, and I entered a Mursi village where a man sat forlorn on a log, doubled over in pain. About 15 feet away the villagers had just slaughtered a cow – a dire act saved for a medical emergency – and they were collecting its blood. The disemboweled bovine splayed across the ground, drawing our horrified fascination. Its stomach spilled out remnants of the bright green grass it must have been chewing just that morning. The villagers repaid our respectful attention by offering us "Mursi coffee" in a worn wooden bowl, which I brought gingerly to my lips for a taste. Spicy strong, Mursi java tasted like a peppery tea, and probably didn't come as a soy latte. After taking his sip, perhaps with less gusto than when sampling a pint of Guinness, Peter was told that the Mursi used the drink as a purgative when their diet of blood and milk proved too rich. The revelation sent a chill of fear and foreboding cascading through his intestinal fortitude.

Yet I digress; let us turn back to our pesky questions. We started with queries about the movements of the people, especially if they had relocated. "Did everybody in your community move, or did some stay?" For those who had left, we probed like pop psychologists on a breezy talk show. "Do you know what happened to them since they left? Do you think they are better or worse off, now, than if they had stayed here?"

Next, we asked how, or whether, the government had consulted the community on moving, and what was promised. The Tsemay people just north of Hamar country complained that the government hadn't provided the iron sheets for roofing their new houses. Even people of the earth knew of the checkered reputation of construction contractors.

We asked how people were moved (trucks, minibus, walking)? We left off beasts of burden. A focus group in Hamar-land said they might use donkeys, or the next best thing – women.

Questions about water and sanitation followed. ("Is water here better or worse than where you were before you moved?) This question became consequential in perhaps our most sad visit, one that the British government tried to keep from being divulged to the public, according to the *Guardian* newspaper. We duly recorded responses about health and education services before shifting to "Livelihoods, food security and land" – possibly the most contentious chunk of our questioning.

About 40 miles west of Turmi on an August day we rumbled through flat terrain. Distant views of plains and mountains framed our journey as we crossed dry stream beds and passed slender, reddish-clay termite towers pointing like crooked fingers skyward. The elegant natural sculptures stood as much as 20 feet tall, as astonishing in their own way as steel skyscrapers raised by human hands.

In these remote grazing lands of the Hamar, shepherd boys carried rifles in case they encountered the Dassanech encroaching with their herds. When rains faltered in these lands, the two peoples sometimes clashed. Paradise had its borders. Researcher Yntiso Gebre had studied the area a few years before and found that drought and dwindling grazing lands were sharpening tensions. Dassanech residents indicated that depleted grazing areas forced them to take their cattle to "risky border places," Gebre wrote in a paper published by the Freie Universitat Berlin. "The Hamar have also been advancing southward to exploit pasture and water in the border areas. Livestock raids/thefts and homicides intensify whenever the two groups converge in the same area."

The government had chosen Kuma for a new village not far from the Omo River, and here there seemed to be real progress. An Ethiopian flag fluttered at the gate of a small work camp. Stacks of pipe suggested that irrigation might be in the offing. A mile away we came upon a set of buildings under construction and stepped out of our vehicles for a look. Peter and Melanie walked around a compact building for classrooms, and nearby what appeared to be a health post. Sneakily I photographed the area guard, a rifle slung over his shoulder. He swung around in annoyance at the sound of the shutter. This was no time for a snapshot of a sentry, guarding a dreamscape.

Who knew whether the Hamar ultimately would settle here, or merely send a few young men to grow maize and sorghum. Yet at least the Ethiopian authorities were trying to get the services lined up before attempting to settle anyone. In parallel, Molloka was promising help with peace building between the Hamar and their neighbors. Could this be the calm heart of the Omo's strife, villagization with a friendly face?

The future farmers would come from Gembela, the last Hamar village as you headed west toward the Omo River. The elders in Gembela said their community had experience only with rain-fed farming and would rely on government "mobilizers" to explain how irrigation planting worked.

In our closing conversation with Molloka a few days later back in Jinka, our companion Patrick of Germany, in his measured yet impatient English-speaking voice, surging and receding, urged the government not to waste this opportunity to build on Hamar goodwill toward the villagization vibe. On our long rides through the valley between villages, Patrick would settle into a deep think, sometimes engrossed in a French novel. He had recently locked in his academic credentials by completing a doctorate in peace and conflict studies focused on the International Criminal Court. As head of the cultural and economic section of the German Embassy in Ethiopia, Herr Patrick looked the part of the rising diplomat of a confident and brainy Deutschland, could shift with ease into diplo-speak and charismatic gravitas, and cut the appealing figure of a future ambassador.

As we discussed during our travel, prospects in Hamar country indeed seemed brighter than in the north near the Omo Kuraz sugar project, where the Mursi held out against the grand plan, fearful of an outright land grab. Hamar communities drew on modest American aid for health care and food security delivered through local organizations, including one run by a retired entrepreneur from Minnesota. In communities between Jinka and Turmi, America's legendary aviation giant Boeing invested a sliver of its stratospheric profits from selling the latest passenger and cargo jets to state-run Ethiopian Airlines, Africa's rising aviation power. Few natives of the Lower Omo Valley had ever seen an airplane, though they may have puzzled over the meaning of thin plumes of vapor traced across their eternal sky.

The paucity of American assistance to this region didn't prevent advocates for Indigenous peoples from targeting the Omo with a powerful weapon fired upon us without warning. The thunderclap caught us in our pajamas.

Sometime in the middle of the night in shivering mid-

January back in Washington, the United States Congress wrapped up a catch-all appropriations measure for fiscal year 2014, aptly named an omnibus bill. Lawmakers dispatched the hulking bill to a final vote in the light of day before anyone could possibly read through it all. This blockbuster hunk of representative democracy celebrated government in action yet also dazzled as legislative sleight of hand. Surprises could be snuggled into a stack of legalese as thick as *War and Peace*.

For our team in Ethiopia the omnibus would prove ominous, for that's how we received the news. The bus clobbered us. On page 525, in section 7042(d), practically a footnote yet still American law in all its stark specificity, there appeared:

Funds appropriated under this Act under the headings 'Development Assistance' and 'Economic Support Fund' that are available for assistance in the lower Omo and Gambella regions of Ethiopia shall:

>   *(A) not be used to support activities that directly or indirectly involve forced evictions;*

>   *(B) support initiatives of local communities to improve their livelihoods; and*

>   *(C) be subject to prior consultation with affected populations.*

The statutory language went on to instruct the United States Treasury Secretary, America's finance minister, to "oppose financing" planned by international financial institutions, such as the World Bank, "for any activities that directly or indirectly involve forced evictions in Ethiopia."

What exactly did "indirectly" mean? While we had found no credible evidence of forced evictions during our spot observation visits, the legal tripwire of offering assistance that might somehow "indirectly" abet nefarious land-grabbing posed a risk not easily dismissed. It would make us cautious about supporting "initiatives" to improve livelihoods if we innocently ended up empowering bad actors. Now it wasn't just the Brits looking over their shoulders for legal rockets as Mursi women raised a ruckus through drooping lips. America suddenly had to tiptoe through the Omo, too.

Only provision (C) gave us cover. Our whole point in doing joint trips into the valley as Ethiopia's international aid givers was to model "prior consultation with affected populations" and encourage the Ethiopian government to do the same. "Free, prior and informed consent" was the emerging human rights formulation. As long as we had eyes on the Omo Valley, and ears open to what the Bodi, Mursi, and Hamar people were thinking aloud, well then forcible evictions, or worse, seemed less likely to take place. Still, there was a growing sense of no way out.

"The team found no evidence of forced migration," we wrote in our report of the trip. "However, it seems clear that the local government and the plantation management have decided that resettlement is necessary." And our discussions showed that the Government of Ethiopia offered communities no viable alternative. "As such the focus of consultation appears to be an effort to persuade the communities to go along with this process, rather than debating options," we noted.

Tasked to define the context for support of activities that "indirectly involve forced evictions," I tried to imagine what would be needed for the removal of populations. Security personnel, whether from local police, regional state forces or federal-level paramilitary or military units, were a probable element given the dangers involved in confronting people likely armed and ready to resist. Transportation, including trucks and possibly boats, would be required. Communications and medical gear and related personnel also plausibly would be involved.

The training or supplying of the coercive actors would be indirectly connected to a forced eviction of communities. I surmised that those actors might include employees of an economic enterprise, private or state-controlled, that stood to benefit from the removal and on whose behalf the state was carrying out the eviction.

In designing and carrying out development aid projects, America would have to be careful to avoid supporting enablers of possible forced evictions. It helped that the United States didn't have much going on or planned in South Omo Zone, apart from my prying eyes, yet American law now ruled this matter. We would have to stay skittish just short of paranoid. Like the overzealous forest invaders of Survival International's tale, poverty-fighting development agencies could end up ejecting people from their homelands with haphazard interventions that aided grasping governments.

Activists in America kept up the heat. A few weeks before I traveled through the valley for the second time, the Oakland Institute issued a report lovingly titled, "Ignoring Abuse in Ethiopia: DFID and USAID in the Lower Omo Valley." Its author was Will Hurd, an American tourist who had grown attached to the Omo after visiting and ended up living with the Mursi for years, long enough to master the language.

Will had put his skills to use translating for an American and British fact-finding trip almost a year before I first stepped into the Omo Valley. His report for Oakland asserted that the representatives of these big donors to the Ethiopian government had heard plenty of disturbing accounts from the locals about coercive practices, yet officially reported that stories of rapes, beatings, and arrests couldn't be substantiated.

"The blind eye turned by USAID and DFID to the human rights violations and forced evictions that accompany the so-called development strategy of Ethiopia is shocking," Will concluded. He insisted that bigger priorities were in play in London and Washington, that Britain and the United States were backing a strategic ally in the Horn of Africa in the face of glaring abuses. "By doing so, they are willful accomplices and supporters of a development strategy that will have irreversible devastating impacts on the environment and natural resources and will destroy the livelihoods of hundreds of thousands of indigenous people."

With such biting accusations swirling around us, my colleagues and I confronted a balancing act. On the one hand, we tried to coax the Ethiopian government to protect the homeland of humanity and the voice and dignity of its inhabitants. On the other hand, we urged Ethiopia to responsibly harness resources including the waters of the Omo to answer our poverty-fighting demands, primarily for energy and food security. Our stated mission as freedom-loving, "Western" governments hinged on preservation of Indigenous cultures as they themselves wished to preserve their ways. We defended communal lands and freedom of choice, having witnessed the upheavals of tyranny by ethnic sorting, from Nazi horrors to Kosovo "cleansing."

The roughshod relocation of Ethiopians from famine-stricken areas of the far north to collective farms in regions to the south by Mengistu's Derg Government during the mid-1980s was not too distant a memory. Coercion carried deadly consequences: As many as 33,000 of these unwilling migrants may have died from hunger as well as malaria and other diseases as they tried to adjust to these unfamiliar settings.

To leave the Omo peoples exposed to overwhelming change without the means to adapt might well make us unwitting conspirators in their misery and exploitation. One afternoon we witnessed the drive-by nature of this phenomenon while visiting with a community of Hamar people under a tree along a roadside, an exposed location unlike most Hamar habitations. Hamar villages tended to sit on high defensive points with gorgeous, sweeping views of the countryside and distant mountains.

Cinematic light bathed these scenes as the sun crept toward the evening horizon. Few visitors made it up into these communities, which could be hard to reach by steep, rutted and rocky dirt roads sometimes reduced to goat paths. Yet the village we had chosen on this day for our fact-finding conversation collected the detritus of road culture. One of the older Hamar adults in the focus group grinned as he showed off a gift from a visitor: his orange construction vest striped with silver reflective tape.

The conversation went on for about an hour, with an earnest exchange of views about development pressures. The government was offering these Hamar residents a new village to the west where they could farm and get health care and schooling more easily, as the pitch went. Yet the Hamar, more savvy than you might expect, hedged their bets. Sure, we'll take your offer, but we'll be keeping our existing villages and grazing lands to see how all of this works out.

We thanked the group for their time, rose and began walking toward our parked vehicles. Just then two Land Cruisers full of camera-toting international tourists screeched to a halt along the road. Within seconds, the Hamar residents who had soberly discussed their communal concerns moments before transformed into a circus troupe. The instant-natives gesticulated and danced as they rushed toward the vehicles. It was Hamar time.

While activists and monitoring tried to keep these peoples somehow untainted by 21st century pressures, the pressures themselves had begun to limit choices and to promote parody. Economic development, energy, market-driven agriculture, educated communities, healthier, longer-living populations protected from disease: these perks of the highlanders would improve the lives of the Hamar and other Omo peoples while tearing their ancient social fabric to pieces.

"Based on our analysis, the pace of sugarcane development and the villagization process in the Omo River [valley] is far faster than the speed at which pastoralists can alter their livelihoods – and worldview," our team wrote.

Isolation still shielded many of these people; for how long, we could not predict. To reach one Hamar village in dry season, we slogged through a sandy, empty riverbed about 75 yards across and came upon men gathered under a clump of trees, passing around sorghum beer in a gourd.

Join us, they said, we just initiated some boys into manhood. A pang of disappointment shot through us. Bull jumping is the signature ritual of the Hamar – for the young man making a literal leap into manhood and for his sister or sisters, who will suffer a harsh beating to show their loyalty to him. The naked adolescent boy must scamper across the backs of several bulls, possibly slicked with dung, back and forth twice, to earn his way into the male fraternity. His sisters, meantime, earn stinging stripes.

As the jumper does his thing, the young women may be whipped with switches until bloody and will have the scars to prove their devotion. There's a masochistic undertone to this practice, which some observers say creates a psychic debt that the boy-man will repay with support for the women in times of trouble. The females nursing their wounds might say the trouble already had begun.

This moment of ritual pride proved to be an awkward time to be carrying out our assessment. We managed to gather a few more-or-less sober men for a focus group and pulled out the questionnaire about resettlement. How long until the next initiation ceremony, we wondered? One of the men took out a string onto which were spaced a series of knots. He began to count these nubs, which we realized marked days. "Hmm," the man said, holding up the knots. "About this long."

Quantifying almost anything – distance, time, number of households – turned into tricky business when interviewing the peoples of the Lower Omo Valley. While a few had made it out into the world beyond for an otherworld education, or received instruction from visiting missionaries, most resided in a cosmos free of the maddening specificity that shapes, controls and ultimately drains meaning from our lives.

A Hamar man offers directions to us in the Lower Omo Valley

"How many households are in this village?" often drew a blank stare from an elder, prompting him to look around helplessly at nearby mud-walled huts. Clearly the Hamar hadn't taken a head count for millennia.

Cattle were quite another matter. The pastoralists had a better sense of how many cows roamed their land – perhaps not down to a number, more in the relative size of the herd. Think of these herds as investments on the move, as long-term savings, your retirement portfolio flowing across the landscape, swatting flies with its tail.

Yet to the north in Omo land, a different herd mentality was taking hold. The chief wrangler, Ato Molloka, could hear the thundering stampede of change on the horizon. When any new idea or innovation comes along, he told us, there will be resistance, in any community. When we brought the villagization idea to the Bodi there were many challenges in persuading them. Likewise, the Mursi were resisting. It doesn't mean they don't have a good relationship with the government.

So impressed were the Mursi skeptics after seeing what the Bodi villages were getting, that the Mursi elders were demanding the same advantages, in Molloka's telling. Time to settle down, they seemed to be thinking. "So nowadays the Mursi are saying, please Molloka, hurry up. Get irrigation to us."

7

Last Days

MANHANDLED TO NOURISH THOUSANDS of acres of sugarcane, the engorged Omo River tumbled downslope and exploded through an improvised gap no wider than a bus is long. On a rise above the turbulence, we stood warily as one of Africa's storied rivers raged against the impudence of mere humans.

Rains had swollen the Omo in a seasonal inundation that had swept tragedy into this same area a few years earlier. That deluge came so fiercely that the river leapt over its banks into villages, killing at least 364 people and displacing as many as 10,000, according to the humanitarian agency of the United Nations.

Relief teams rushed supplies to the scene. Thirty-seven tons of grain, medicines, and 1,000 blankets arrived for the victims. However, reaching the survivors proved tough. "The area is inaccessible by road," noted a United Nations bulletin. "The response is difficult due to the remoteness of the area affected."

That lethal flood erupted in mid-August. Eight years later I stood with my travel colleagues on another mid-August day, agog at this less threatening though still raw display of natural power. The Omo churned and leaped, twisting and slashing through the chokepoint with animal force as gravity drove the cascade down toward the sprawling Omo Kuraz sugar plantation glinting in sunlight.

Spent and liberated, the caramel flow settled down and rejoined the becalmed natural course a few hundred yards away. Curving away through the primeval landscape, the Omo slipped out of view beneath mountains ornamenting the western sky, bound for Kenya.

Omo waters nurtured Ethiopia's grand ambition. The great sugar project grew ever larger as early fields of cane and the factories and work camps that came along with the impending test harvest spread across the site. The revelations had only begun. Ato Molloka's shenanigans with our translators the previous year had curtailed our visits to communities near the sugarcane plantation, so my German colleague Patrick and I, joined by David, a genial Spaniard from the European Union, had made a point to come out west on this excursion. Peter had left Ethiopia for new exploits back home.

Along a tree-shaded stream near a Bodi village, we watched as young men uncloaked, revealing hard-muscled torsos and not so much as a pinch of fat. The men immersed in the flow, washing themselves, then withdrew dark, glistening bodies from the waters. A dog cooled himself mid-stream, contented. On the riverbank, the bathers pulled on tunics of blue, purple, and emerald.

Later in the day, as dusk gathered near the plantation, the romantic imagery faded. We came upon the crude villagization site called Kokilomeri and a small group of distressed Bodi women. They said the government had brought them there two years earlier and told them to stay. We observed rudimentary tukuls in a confined, muddy area in the bush. The women reported suffering from bloody diarrhea from unsafe water fetched from the irrigation canal. They complained of mosquitos and the threat of malaria, and of headaches of unspecified origin. Health care was an eight-hour walk back to the town of Hana, the women said. Their children didn't go to school. The area was "barely habitable," the worst conditions we had seen on the Omo Kuraz plantation, we noted in our on-the-spot report. These "isolated and vulnerable" people appeared to be there to provide a token presence on an unfit site. They needed to be moved.

The British government would twice reject freedom of information requests to release our report, which included this discovery at Kokilomeri, saying it could "significantly damage," U.K. interests, according to the *Guardian* newspaper. The European Commission subsequently handed over the report to Survival International.

Darkness settled over the Omo waters and the first-phase fields of sugarcane. Rattled by our discovery at Kokilomeri, up we went to the hilltop nerve center of this battle of nerves. At the end of a long day of field research, our team had converged on the Omo Kuraz construction headquarters. In a conference room we joined the general manager, planners, consultants, Sugar Corp officials and local government functionaries for an early evening briefing.

On one wall a map glowed like an electronic guide to another galaxy. Lines in green, purple and blue, demarcating plots of land, new towns, canals, roads, and reserves for resettled pastoralists danced in the firmament as the general manager moved a crosshair target across a screen. The visual represented a detailed schematic diagram of the master plan for the Omo Kuraz sugar project, Ethiopia's biggest ever bet on big agriculture. We sat back in fascination as the details began to form an overwhelming picture.

The general manager moved his target over the schematic, describing how 50 worker towns would spring up, each with about 2,000 residents. Each of the planned sugar factories – where raw cane was crushed and squeezed to extract juice and boiled to crystallize into sugar – would have its own town of at least 5,000 people.

Fifty towns? How many people might be on this sprawling site at peak production, we wondered. With crisp satisfaction the Sugar Corp planners estimated that all told perhaps 500,000 might settle into this area during the temporary surge of workers for the harvest. That was more than twice the number of Indigenous Omo inhabitants. The Mursi, Bodi and other communities would have to take a number just to get served.

In an instant our image of the change coming to the Omo Valley flipped from thousands of acres of sweet grass marching along the banks of the Omo River, crowding out some plodding cattle herds, to a wave of urban settlement stripping away the Omo ethos for all time. Sugar Corp then made a startling admission. The Indigenous communities in the Omo knew nothing about the number of planned towns for workers. Consultations with the Omo's rooted residents had neglected to mention the human tsunami bearing down on them.

Already we had observed signs of the ugly to come. A workers' settlement had arisen along a stretch of plantation road. Black mud sucked at the wheels of our vehicles as we passed. An Ethiopian town was rarely pleasing to the eye, something of a jumble, and this encampment tilted toward that same scrambled look, only far less tamed.

I thought: these sugar-mad people, no aesthetic instincts, no sense of pleasing order. Houses and shops made of woven fiber walls in monochromatic style crammed into the area. Two men played ping pong across from a yard full of beefy Chinese trucks. The Omo Kuraz site in full swing would be quite the improvised eyesore, though one that few outsiders would see, so deep was this urban outbreak in the wilds of Ethiopia. Yet modernity would slither into this once pristine landscape in all its guises. Shabby shops, belching vehicles, boisterous bars, slipshod restaurants, greasy repair depots, and possibly a vast sex trade would spread from these towns. The health implications alone sounded alarms.

The Mursi skeptics of Hailewuha indeed had much to worry them. The briefing revealed that the Mursi would be moved to a new area south of the plantation's "command area" near the Omo. When we later visited Romos, a resettlement village intended for Mursi near the sugar plantation, an elder of the Bodi people with snake-like scars on his forearm and brass earrings resembling rock-climbing clips wondered how traditional ways would survive.

Looking in the direction of a ramshackle construction camp about 500 yards away, the elder asked who had invited the Chinese in to build on our land. If more Mursi arrive, where will our cattle graze? Bringing herds together isn't our culture. And what if more outsiders settle here? The elder paused after spitting into the dirt. There will be shooting.

Later that afternoon in another village, Mursi elders of higher rank sketched a tougher line. The government had asked them to resettle in three communities near the Omo, including the proto-village Romos from which we had just come. The sugar project is overrunning our land, clear-cutting trees, and reducing our grazing areas, we heard. The government says you should have fewer cattle and is telling us to move, or they will "take by power," said one.

Another elder, tall with white-disk earrings, said he was shown the Bodi villages on the sugar plantation. Everything was cleared, no trees remained for shade, the elder lamented. He heard that crocodiles in the irrigation canal had attacked Bodi children playing in the water. A man in his 30s joined in the discussion, saying the community is watching what's happening in Romos. "We want you to send a letter to different governments to stop this site," he said. We would like the schools and health care that the government is offering, he added, if workers aren't settled among us.

Finally, an older man at the head of the group began to speak. Oddly he wore a T-shirt with 16 "feelings" faces and the Spanish phrase: *"Como te sientes hoy?"* The man said he had visited Japan and that the Oxford anthropologist David Totten had lived with him. This was the spiritual leader of the Mursi in this northern region of the Omo Valley. All cattle fell under his sway, our translator explained.

We are nomads, we move freely, the leader observed. He listed the fears: government pressure, the degradation of the ecosystem, and worst of all, being settled adjacent to antagonistic tribes. He claimed that in messages and in meetings, the government threatened to send in security forces to beat the Mursi if they wouldn't move to Romos.

Could the Mursi live with the sugar project, we wondered?

Yes, if the government gives us land to farm and shows us how, the vulnerable venerable one opined.

The culture and way of life of the Mursi and Bodi peoples are likely to be "fundamentally and irreversibly transformed in the near future," our team later reported. Turton made the same point on his Mursi Online site. "If these plans are realized, not only will the lower Omo become by far the largest irrigation complex in Ethiopia, but the resident population of agro-pastoralists will be transformed into wage laborers and sedentary cultivators. This will involve a resettlement program which, although described as 'voluntary,' will be forced, in the sense that those affected will have no reasonable alternative but to comply."

Wildlife would have to make room for sugar dreams, too. During our briefing at the sugar plantation headquarters, the crosshair target rolled across the screen, and another layer of the schematic materialized. Omo Kuraz plantation will "jump" the 1,500-square-mile Omo National Park, the briefer explained, with only the irrigation canal and road running through the reserve. A 25-mile wildlife corridor would extend north to south, allowing antelope and pachyderm alike to move through their habitat sugar-free, at least in theory. The plan called for bridges spanning the irrigation canal so animals could meander across like tourists.

A few years earlier, an aerial and ground survey of Omo National Park by African Parks Ethiopia, a conservation group, had found small herds of elephant, buffalo, and giraffe, perhaps two dozen lions and a range of smaller animals including hartebeest and lesser kudu. The most abundant populations counted in the research were of tiang and eland, antelope species numbering about 2,000 each within the park. With its grassy plains, woody savanna hills, and forested mountains, the Omo National Park hosted more than 300 bird species and 57 of mammals, some depleted to almost pitiful stragglers, others counted in appreciable herds. Of greater importance, the Omo refuge connected with a larger ecosystem stretching into the western Gambella region of Ethiopia and eventually across the border into Sudanese backcountry. I gave the sugar planners credit for considering the broader biodiversity implications of their agro ambitions. Perhaps more credit than I would give for their sympathies toward sapiens.

"The Omo National Park is a huge and dynamic ecological and ethnical system with communities having their social and economic structure closely linked with natural resources utilization," African Parks Ethiopia reported.

Zebras looked longingly at the park and would be most intrigued by the envisioned wildlife bridges. The surveyors found that Africa's equine dazzlers were stranded on the east bank of the Omo in herds totaling around 2,400 animals. The Bodi in that area left them alone. As surveyors methodically flew transects across the park about 300 feet above the ground, spotters tallied more formidable natural interlopers: humans and their livestock. Cattle, along with sheep and goats ("shoats" to livestock counters), outnumbered all the wild beasts by 10 to 1 when surveyors counted within the Omo National Park and in an adjacent buffer area.

Cattle roamed in the tens of thousands and consequently were chewing up the landscape, especially in the southern reaches of the area populated by the Nyangatom people. "Land pressure due to the need to access water and grazing areas appears to be very high," the African Parks report observed. "This is a major issue and is very apparent with the Nyangatom who seem to have very few other options of where to water and graze their large numbers of cattle other than going north into the park or west into Suri land."

Chasing the setting sun leads to danger. Known for their warrior ethos, the Suri live on undulating savanna west of the Omo River and north of Lake Turkana in the borderland of Ethiopia and South Sudan. The agro-pastoralist Suri also need space and grass for their cattle, adding pressure on the park and yet another reason to set their facial mode to fierce. Violent and deadly confrontations multiplied in the area.

The startling pointillist face paint designs of the Suri function as a magnet for photographers – and a frightful repellent for foes. Integral to Suri culture, especially of the major sub-group known as Chai, is a sort of devotion to violence, both in self-defense against cattle raiders and to assert domination as a quality of manhood, according to researcher Jon Abbink. Chai means, "We revenge."

A national park invaded by cattle and shoats and home to a few lonely lions, giraffes, and elephants seemed like a poor candidate for buffing into a wildlife haven for rich safari tourists. Yet that's exactly what African Parks had in mind, with the deep pockets of a Dutch billionaire underwriting the paradisal vision.

Paul Fentener van Vlissingen had tapped wealth from his family's business interests in oil, gas, scrap-metal recycling, and retailing to buy an 80,000-acre, road-less estate in the Scottish Highlands in 1978 as a conservation area. The poetry-writing tycoon opened his land to public use by hikers and climbers in exchange for adherence to responsible conduct. "He brought to land management problems the Dutch tradition of dialogue and constructive debate," the *Independent* newspaper wrote on his passing in 2006 from cancer at 65 years old.

An avid outdoorsman, Van Vlissingen sometimes would head off into the Scottish wilderness on a pony saddled with a week's provisions. No doubt a few lines of poetry trotted through his thoughts along the way. When South African liberator Nelson Mandela challenged the environmentalist 20 years after his Scottish foray to revive Africa's neglected parks, Van Vlissingen agreed to plunge into remote, whisky-free terrain. Scottish hikers and herders turned out to be far easier to handle than the tenacious inhabitants of Africa's more seductive landscapes, including the Lower Omo Valley.

The billionaire hired Shauna, the Canadian anthropologist then doing field research, to help with the startup. Van Vlissingen poured money in to buy vehicles and crank up the conservation effort with local and international staff. A vision of a thriving wildlife sanctuary began to take shape in this remote corner of Ethiopia. Too soon, the optimal scenario faded. Bipedal beings trampled the African Parks dream as surely as hoofed gastronomes devoured the delectable grasses in the park. A Dutch dream of harmony with nature, it turns out, would be uprooted on the way to that tenacious Dutch legacy – an obsession with sugar.

African Parks could not gain the government's support or trust, or perhaps both, to act as a broker of wise natural stewardship. Activists complained that efforts to gazette Omo National Park – that is, to set legal boundaries for the conservation area - would deprive the traditional residents of grazing and farming. They would become "illegal squatters" on their land. Two years after signing a management agreement with the Government of Ethiopia, African Parks called it quits in the Lower Omo Valley.

"Our actions were based on the fact that the only chance of securing a sustainable future for Omo and the people dependent on the ecosystem was negotiating limits of use of the land and natural resources by each one of the different ethnic groups," said African Parks in a public statement. "If successful this would have ensured the long-term sustainability of sections of the Park, and the creation of community conservation areas in others. It would also have brought about regional peace and stability, something desired by all the ethnic groups."

African Parks accused human rights activists of targeting its management effort "without ever visiting the area and consulting with the very communities whose interests they purported to represent."

"We do not believe that African Parks can solve the complexities of Omo, at least not in the time frame anticipated," the organization concluded. "To continue is simply a waste of scarce resources which can be better applied elsewhere."

Looking back on that time, Shauna calls Van Vlissengen's death "a tragedy for the world of conservation and for the Omo Valley." Had African Parks carried out its plans, she says, the sugar plantation would not have encroached on national park lands, and the pastoralists would have counted on more supporters with the influence to defend their cause.

Mago National Park to the east also looked likely to join the land squeeze. With an epic sugarcane sprawl on the way, towns proliferating, wild animals trying to hold their ground, herders searching for shrinking grazing lands, and the potential for more tourists to punch tickets at a Paleolithic human zoo, the Omo Valley seemed likely to get more crowded than the Creator ever imagined.

These thoughts weighed on us as we arrived at our quarters for the night – the residential compound of the Chinese engineers working on the plantation's vast irrigation system, the spigot supplied by the Omo River itself. We chatted up the 30-something managers, pleasant and well versed in English. They lamented that their assignment in the Ethiopian wilderness offered few diversions, not even satellite television.

In the artificial light cutting through the deep darkness, a menagerie of strange insects whirled and buzzed. Then I heard what sounded like a hurled baseball smack into the window of the dormitory. I spun around and shuddered. The projectile turned out to be an airborne Omo insectoid of unknown vintage and suspect navigational skills. Nature both primordial and ruthlessly modern seemed on the loose out here, eager to keep a visitor on edge.

Where, we wondered, might there be a model of integrated development to free us from this binary choice between an agricultural dream on steroids and preserving the Indigenous way of life in an impoverished Stone Age reserve?

I've got one, suggested Ato Molloka, his mode set to maximum community-action mobilizer.

Wait, what? We spun in his direction.

The Mursi people of Maki already live along a river at some distance east of the sugar plantation and had proposed to "villagize in place," he had told us while we sat in his office in Jinka. Instead of moving that Mursi community as first discussed with elders, the government decided to keep those folks exactly where they resided and to build an expanded Mursi settlement around them. An irrigation scheme would bring waters of the Maki River into farm plots. Maki had the geographic advantage of sitting just far enough from the gravitational pull of the Omo Kuraz project to stay intact.

As we investigated this area, the editors of the Journal of Human Evolution were preparing an article on the Omo Mursi Formation, described as "a window on the East African Pliocene." This epoch extended from about 2.5 million to 5.3 million years ago. The Mursi Formation, on the east bank of the Omo River southwest of Maki, dates to more than 4 million years ago, and is one of four major fossil-bearing geologic formations in the Lower Omo Valley of world importance to understanding human evolution in context. Taken together these sites are "the only place in the world to have continuously and accurately recorded the environmental changes and faunal evolution that accompanied the appearances of the first stone tools" of humankind, according to an Ethiopian government submission to the World Heritage Committee of the United Nations.

The journal article by anthropologist Michelle Drapeau of the University of Montreal and collaborators talked of a new fossil site in the formation called Chola. Well preserved remains of pigs, hogs, and boars dominate, with a lesser concentration of bovids.

In Pliocene times, the global climate cooled and became more arid, which promoted the spread of grasslands. Grazing animals became larger and more capable of covering large distances to reach new feeding areas. During the Pliocene, "apes came down from trees and started to exist on the plains in Africa," explains the University of California Museum of Paleontology. "In fact, it is generally believed that *Australopithecus* evolved in the late Pliocene."

The most famous Australopithecus, or "Southern Ape," emerged in fragments from the rich fossil layers of the Afar desert in northern Ethiopia in 1974 thanks to the eagle eyes of a young American paleoanthropologist, Donald Johanson. Fate named this diminutive, 3.2-million-year-old woman Lucy, after a Beatles song playing at Johanson's field camp. (The senior Ethiopian official on the scene conferred an Amharic cognomen, "Dinkinesh" – "You are marvelous.") Lucy, officially *Australopithecus afarensis*, would become the most famous hominid discovery of the 20th century, celebrated in journals, magazines and movies into the 21st.

I had the good fortune to meet and chat with Johanson in Addis Ababa and celebrate with him as he welcomed Lucy back from a years-long tour in America. (And shortly after, I took advantage of the rare chance to examine this extraordinary hominid from inches away through glass at the National Museum in Addis, before she went back into the vault.) This landmark discovery owed much to Johanson's first African fieldwork – in the Omo Valley, as I later learned. From 1967 to 1970 a remarkable grouping of scientists converged on the valley for an intensive examination of its history under the banner of the International Omo Research Expedition.

The aging French wunderkind Camille Arambourg was there, decades after his first Omo exploration in 1933. Arambourg's interest in deep time was sparked in his 20s by the fossil fishes plowed up on his father's farm in Algeria. Richard Leakey, son of the British-Kenyan scientist Louis Leakey, who made remarkable fossil finds around Lake Turkana, led the Kenyan contingent. And from the University of Chicago came F. Clark Howell, who invited his student Johanson on his first trip to Africa for work as an assistant.

The fossil treasures of the Omo Mursi Formation remind us of the unimaginably long story of this consequential valley. Of forgotten quests, agonizing trials and cherished triumphs in the journey leading to our species and our era. And yet, there is continuity, across long years. Grasslands thread through time, a million seasons, and have worked their way into the fiber of our human story.

Anchoring the Maki-Orachaga community was a missionary school that taught English and basic skills and exposed Mursi youth to the world beyond while maintaining respect for their traditions. Might Maki be the key to solving the developmental riddle of the Lower Omo Valley? We determined to find out.

One fine morning our high-clearance vehicles splashed across the sparkling, shallow Maki River, our drivers turning nimbly this way and that to keep the waters from gushing into our floorboards. The current tugged at our rolling metal, yet our rugged tires held, and we gained traction on the far shore. Up on dry land, the elders were waiting for us. The elders said they had not yet decided whether to accept the government's expansion plan. Instead, they were watching and waiting as the government constructed buildings for services. The elders seemed uninformed about the scope of this construction, which seemed strange given its proximity to Orachaga – maybe 800 yards away.

"Because the land belongs to the community, they must come and talk to us," one elder said of the government's men. My notes from that day reflect the mist of ignorance that seemed to hang over this village: "The community has not/not been shown a map of area development by the Government of Ethiopia, so their grasp of the scale of changes confronting Maki seems limited. At the same time, the elders seem disengaged from the facts on the ground just a short walk away."

Highlander construction workers were putting the finishing touches on an eight-room school for grades five through eight. Children who completed the mission-run primary school could then continue their education in these higher grades. Up the hill, housing for teachers was ready. Nearby stood a new health post along with a veterinary clinic, with a corral for treating cattle. The cinder block structures seemed uncommonly well made, with downspouts, outdoor lighting, and pleasing paint colors.

Unpaved roads cut through the bush in a grid, connecting the school and clinics, and suggesting that a much larger settlement indeed was on the way. Perhaps the elders simply wished these harbingers of a world profoundly changed to go away. Denial kept their authority safely intact and somehow unchallenged.

Among the young men of the community, blunter passions came to the fore. Standing around us, muscled, with AK-47s slung over shoulders, these men came across as warriors with a manifesto. Confronting the government's pressures, they spelled out three red lines: don't take our guns, don't touch our grazing land, and don't move other peoples onto our territory.

As our conversations in this transformative community ended and we stowed our pens, a table and tablecloth appeared. Soon the chef that my European colleagues had ferried from Addis along with a vehicle packed with provisions began bringing out a spread of food for lunch. For a moment the humble village transformed into a gourmet cooking show in a sun-dappled clearing with the Maki murmuring nearby.

By now the myriad thoughts of this journey had begun to sift in our minds. It was time to head back to Ato Molloka, the center of gravity of Ethiopian authority in this fabled valley. At five minutes before 5 in the afternoon, the South Omo Zone headquarters came to life with the Castilian-inflected English of our team leader from the European Union, Senor David.

Beyond the Omo Valley the world seemed especially unsettled that day. In West Africa, governments and health workers scrambled to contain the largest known outbreak of the lethal Ebola virus, which threatened to ravage rural populations. In Eurasia, the deadly epidemic was of old-school nationalism as Ukrainian forces battled pro-Russian separatists supported by Russian military power. Mother Nature and Mother Russia sought to forcibly evict people from their land through blood.

"We have detected a significant risk of conflict in the future" because of the fear that large numbers of highlanders will be coming to live on the land of the native Omo peoples, David announced. Pay attention to how to manage conflict, he advised. In tone and urgency, this message from our team departed from the past debriefs of Molloka, which centered on stepping up consultations and delivering better services. That messaging seemed almost quaint now. The highlanders were coming like an invading force, one that promised a jolt of prosperity to the valley, though with the significant likelihood of a forever type of disruption.

While the people of the Omo desire access to health care, veterinary services for their cattle and safe water, David continued, they don't accept having those services at any price. Cattle and grazing land carry high value. So too does the cultural integrity of these ancient peoples.

For Molloka, too, something had changed. We've consulted with the pastoralists for four years, we've assured them that no one is touching their grazing land, he protested with a measure of weariness. Even when we want to villagize them, a committee will be formed, and they will choose the village site. I was appointed to this position three years ago, Molloka reminded us. Delegates from embassies and from different organizations have visited. These communities should be given support for health, water, and schools. I've seen visits go back and forth. "What is your plan to change the lives of the people?" he queried.

Patrick asserted on behalf of his ambassador that the Mursi need a slower pace to adapt. The government should help the pastoralists maintain their traditional lifestyle for as long as necessary. This American noted that consultations have reached a point where the pastoralists need concrete action to make the talks productive, give them new life and confidence. I added that Maki might be the place where that happens. David built on this theme. We need a participatory effort to help communities that want to find a middle way on villagization, one that meets their needs. We also suggested, perhaps too meekly, that the Ethiopians needed to seek best practices from around the world to deal with problems sure to arise, including crime, disease, and prostitution.

As we paused, Ato Molloka turned reflective, chiseling in air what might become the credo for a vanished world. "We have set the pastoralists free from their backwardness."

"If we had used force to move these people, we could have done it during the first year, 2011. It would be very easy, because the government has power, but we chose another option. We know it's a new lifestyle, so we set about to convince them. As a country, our economy is growing fast, so we are changing fast."

Ethiopia has signed onto the United Nations-approved Millennium Development Goals for education, which obligates us to bring education to every child, even pastoralists, Molloka continued. They say our girls can't go to school, but we want all kids in school, so we have to convince them gradually.

Molloka had backed us into a corner that we had fashioned ourselves, in neat angles. Ethiopia had agreed to follow our demands for building a world ever freer of disease, hunger, and ignorance. Who were we then to call out Ethiopia for trying to carry out that mandate across its population? Where was the border between progress for the masses and stubborn protection of the past?

As if the passage of time itself was at stake, the United Nations planners had decreed that by the 15th year of the 21st century as we counted the circumambulation of our planet around our local star, the world would arrive at a watershed moment for global poverty, benchmarked to the Millennium goals. Ethiopia's disciplined political cadre took this competition as seriously as any race on the planet, as if loping to the finish line for gold and world-beating accolades in feats of long-distance running. In this global development game as in Olympian contests of long strides, the Ethiopians truly did grab a large share of glory.

"Today Ethiopia celebrates the fact that the proportion of people below the poverty line has been halved; the prevalence of hunger and undernourishment has been reduced; access to education has expanded; the gap in enrollment between boys and girls has narrowed; under-five mortality has been reduced by two-thirds; and similar progress was recorded in reducing HIV/AIDS, malaria, tuberculosis and other diseases," trumpeted a joint report from the United Nations and the Ethiopian National Planning Commission.

On the energy front, Ethiopia turned out to be that shining student who proudly turns in her homework on the appointed day. "A Climate Resilient Green Economy Strategy has been formulated and the Government has set itself a bold vision of becoming a middle-income carbon-neutral economy by 2025," the UN marveled.

To the scorecard we go. Of the eight goals, Ethiopia achieved six, according to the assessment, including: universal primary education; reducing child mortality; combating HIV/AIDS, malaria, and other diseases; ensuring environmental sustainability; and developing a "global partnership for development" – taking in billions of dollars from other governments yet spending the largesse on pro-poor services that created jobs and pumped up long-term economic growth.

The UN's claim that Ethiopia had notched a sixth win by eradicating "extreme poverty and hunger" went too far. While many fewer Ethiopians were struggling with dire poverty and empty stomachs compared with two decades earlier, a gathering drought was about to slam Ethiopia with a full-blown hunger crisis. It would become a stark reminder of the country's climatic vulnerability. Failed rains due to El Nino weather patterns would require emergency food aid for 10 million Ethiopians, including almost a half-million malnourished children, as crop production tumbled 90 percent in some areas and hundreds of thousands of livestock perished. The vast hunger did not spare the Lower Omo Valley.

Ethiopia's report card revealed other low marks. In promoting gender equality and women's empowerment, Ethiopia flopped. Early marriage, violence against girls, and education gaps conspired to rebuff Ethiopia in this contest of wills. Out beyond Addis Ababa, the male domain held firm with fierce, leonine pride. Maternal health also proved to be an unfinished quest as rural and tradition-bound regions resisted the international push for care by skilled health workers during pregnancy. Yet for a nation that had emerged from feudal mists during the preceding century of turbulent change, the future spoke with uncommon clarity and resolve.

Yet did the past have a future?

Already Molloka spoke of building a "big" museum of Omo cultures in Jinka costing 200 million Ethiopian birr – about 10 million dollars at the time, a fantastic sum in a spartan land. The museum, we were promised, would host researchers and anthropologists along with a stream of camera-loving tourists.

Would the Valley of the Lower Omo be reduced to a time capsule, to be pulled out and dusted off every so often as reminder of what once was, yet never again would be? In the homeland of humanity, would we find no one at home? Were these the last days in this valley beyond all valleys?

8

A Frontier Closing

IMPOSSIBLY DISTANT SUNS PRICKED our cosmic ceiling with the startling clarity and profusion of a planetarium show, though none of the hushed awe.

Drumbeats and singing hurled heavenward as a throng of men and women jostled around a roaring fire. From my seated vantage point, through an undulating pack of sinewy torsos, I could detect bodies jerking upward like pogo sticks around the fiery inner glow. Airborne and joyful, this Hamar village had come together at our invitation and with our gratitude for gleefully enabling us to meddle in their affairs.

Off to the side across a clearing a smaller, equally intense blaze beckoned, tended by five men bent to their task, bathed in billowing warm hues. Dancing would not be dancing without the promise of feasting. As a gift to the village, our team had pooled 250 dollars and purchased an unsuspecting cow. We checked that off our shopping list and stepped aside. Nimble hands aided by night-vision eyes butchered the beast in the enfolding dusk. When the light vanished, I strolled over in the kinetic darkness to observe the Stone Age gourmands and their approach to outdoor grilling.

At once I was flung back millennia. During how many nights of lost ages had children crouched spellbound at the edge of that flickering veil of heat? From a rectangular pit issued a hissing blaze, coals pulsating in volcanic reds and oranges. About one yard away stood a vertical rack fashioned from sturdy tree branches, resembling the antlers of an elk. Thick slabs of cow parts nestled into this frame, cooking ever so slowly. By morning, not so much as a bone would be left in the clearing. No organic salad here. No potatoes mashed or crinkled. This was carnivore country, a pure paradise of paleo protein. An authentic greet and meat.

Over at the edge of the exuberant crowd sat a middle-aged guy toting a beefy torso crowned by a sagging Boston Red Sox baseball cap. He entertained Hamar kids by flicking his lighted watch face on and off in the darkness, his grin widening as their eyes bulged and sparkled. In no-tech country, a blazing wrist appeared to be the work of a visiting conjurer.

In his vast world, some may have thought so. Brian had ventured beyond the tangible, specific now into the spirit territory of peoples tethered to a deep and otherworldly existence. Along Amazon waters, out under the stars with the San hunter-gatherers in the southern African desert or among the rain-forest tribes of Papua New Guinea struggling to survive the invasive mining of gold, copper, and nickel. While quaffing a draft beer from a bar stool, Brian would marvel at these keepers of deep time and portals into fantastic worlds, stewards of land and sacred spaces under threat from a brash, bustling, and impatient world.

Brian's neighbors in Boston could scarcely imagine the secretive Indigenous cosmos he explored. Possibly they knew Brian only as an amateur boxer, jabbing away in a neighborhood ring back in the day. His treasured friends – for Brian commanded respect among Indigenous communities around the planet – held dear their repositories of human knowledge in a world enthralled by shallow and ephemeral exhibitions.

The Congress had decreed that America would hire an adviser on Indigenous affairs to inform and guide global development work. Brian became the first to hold the job. He would use this special position, reporting to the Administrator of the United States Agency for International Development, to push the White House to get behind native peoples in their struggle against economic encroachment of their lands. Indeed, the name of Brian's advocacy group said it all: Land Is Life. Brian urged the United States Government under a President of African descent to bring these time-tested voices to the table in the design and evaluation of American foreign-aid programs. The urging took a while; the business of ancients always did.

As a pandemic began to squeeze the planet in 2020, exactly 130 years after the head of the United States Census Bureau declared that the blanket incursion of white settlers had forever erased America's Indian frontier, Washington issued an international development policy for Indigenous communities. The act itself astonished; swirling all around in America were aggrieved Caucasian antagonists battling waves of ethnic and racial invaders tinted mocha, caramel, and copper, rather than red, white, and blue.

The Indigenous peoples existing seen and unseen across the planet, neither living fossils nor clueless hermits, numbered in the hundreds of millions. While safeguarding the received wisdom of the ages, they found themselves as contemporary passengers of Mother Earth in the dark ocean of the Milky Way.

"Indigenous Peoples are stewards of a wide range of critical ecosystems, and of much of the earth's biological diversity," the policy reminded us. "Their livelihoods and traditional resource-management strategies are among the most sustainable."

The policy laid out four objectives: engage with Indigenous populations to safeguard them from harm and encourage self-reliance; integrate Indigenous concerns across American development investments; empower Indigenous peoples to "practice self-determined development;" and foster conditions for these people to advocate for and claim their rights.

Brian came to Ethiopia with Washington experts fascinated

by the dignity and determination of African pastoralists. Oren, 60-something polymath with degrees in theoretical mathematics, French and finance, had crossed the street from investment banking to become the senior adviser to America's top development official in Africa.

Walter, a lanky, bearded research scientist and senior environmental adviser, bore a slender frame poised to balance a fishing rod or a camera tripod. And Leslie, the point person on international development loans, pondered the environmental impact of projects that might be financed with American tax dollars.

As we traversed the roads of Hamar country, the Agency for International Development was finishing up "Operational Guidelines for Responsible Land-Based Investment." Published four months later in Washington, the guide aimed to help corporate investors understand that land wasn't simply up for grabs in Africa like a conquistador's new worlds for the taking. Instead, rather resourceful Africans resided in those hills, fields, and forests.

Investment in land was rising as more companies jostled to satisfy global demand for food, biofuel, wood, and horticultural products. Global population was rising; choice land was shrinking. Yet this stampede to acquire land came with a big downer: land tenure risk. Is anyone home out here? The reply quite often reverberated: Well, yes. And: Who are you?

"Although Africa is routinely cited as the location with the greatest amount of uncultivated arable land in the world, it is important for investors to understand that most land in Africa is not empty," the report's authors felt obligated to point out. "On the contrary, it is often home to – or used by – groups of local people who have occupied the land for generations, even centuries."

Responsible investors should respect the rights of the people on the land, rights that often arise out of customary practices, the authors counseled. "Whenever possible, investors should consider avoiding the large-scale transfer of tenure rights and look for alternatives that limit harm to local communities, such as contract farming and out-grower schemes" in which farmers supply crops to a food company. The operational guidelines ended on an upbeat note evocative of our entreaties to Molloka: the goal of investments in land should be "to find positive outcomes for all affected parties."

Let's ponder this cheerful American take on the travails of the weary African Indigenous time traveler. How to find those outcomes in a world of big governments and even bigger global markets? Why, "stakeholder engagement," of course. An entire chapter touched the subject, with suggestions on how to link up with local traditional leaders with their fingers on the pulse of land issues. In some cases, of course, these chiefs and elders had their fingers curled around goodies for themselves.

On the issue of land, everyone seemed to have a sense of the frontier closing, even on a continent as sprawling and "empty" as Africa.

As Walter viewed it, pastoralism wasn't fading out, just misunderstood, and deserving of fresh appreciation. As a long-term livelihood strategy, pastoralism amounted to an admirable, sustainable way of life – if only maddening modernity would slow down and take a closer look. Critical to making pastoralism thrive in the hyper-competitive 21st century was mobility. That meant being able to move herds to rain-fed areas under the protection of customary institutions that police the use of communal grasslands.

Yet mobility might be powerless to help pastoralists find fodder for their cattle and ample food for their families when the skies simply refused to release water. During our wanderings in the Omo Valley, the neighboring Borena region of Ethiopia to the east along the border with Kenya was suffering from the highest annual rainfall deficits since the middle of the 20th century. While grasslands withered, researchers cultivated a thicket of terminology to assess the plight of these pastoralists, the most attention-grabbing of which was "shock exposure."

A cascade of livelihood "shocks" jarred the pastoral scene. Loss of prized livestock cut household income, which in turn reduced the consumption of nutritious food such as milk, and emptied money pouches meant to pay school fees and to repay loans. Illness and malnutrition increased among children. The dry earth trembled with consequence for these communities.

There were "conflict shocks" too as desperation spread – people stealing cattle and crops, and violence against household members. Researchers looked at 20 factors that together measured "resilience," defined as the ability to recover from shocks – from social capital to cash savings to humanitarian assistance. In the face of extreme climate changes, resilience became a kind of incantation against shifting natural forces.

During a four-year period that coincided with our visits to the Omo, the share of Borena households consuming less food as a coping strategy in the face of drought jumped to nine in 10 from seven in 10. Pastoralists came to rely on aid in food and cash simply to survive. Once more the arid reality of scarcity intruded. The reassuring vision of noble herders thriving across a timeless sea of grass seemed to blow away in the parched Ethiopian wind.

To the west of Borena, the clever Hamar fared better, as we found in our field visit. Starting at about 4,000 feet in altitude, our vehicles fought uphill over a rocky road reduced to a walking path, gaining about 1,500 feet as the valley fell away and a mountaintop loomed. Lush grassy slopes and thick trees carpeted the mountainsides as the stony path leveled out into a village.

Around noon about 20 men ranging in age from 30s to 50s waited on a hill next to a storybook acacia tree, its delicate canopy completing the bucolic scene. Almost 2,000 people lived up here in harmony with a forest. The Minnesota entrepreneur's charitable organization helped with communal management skills to protect the trees. An elder related that neighboring villages had come to learn about the approach. If only these trees could talk.

Population growth, the need for new land as young men married and started families, the use of fire to collect forest honey, and cutting large trees for houses – all pressured the viability of the forest cover. Hamar country seemed little different than Ethiopia at large, where forests had dwindled since the 1950s. Tree hugging might be the only way left to fend off the hordes: in the past generation alone, Ethiopia's population had doubled.

Alas, a livestock challenge loomed. This Hamar community's cattle grazed a four days' walk away in Mago National Park, stirring up trouble. Park guards didn't like it, and neither did the Mursi nearby. From time to time, conflict erupted.

Yet forests, grasses, and cattle didn't stir passions quite like what was happening in the schools. The chief elder said in many villages over the years, armed government officials had taken elders as "hostages" when a community resisted sending their children to the government schools. Threats and intimidation swirled in this battle of wits. Across the world, from North America to Australia, stories surfaced of the unforgiving tactics that the predominant culture had deployed in schools to harness Indigenous youth to the heroic task of nation building.

As we headed west one day from Turmi toward the fabled Omo River, a cotton farm fluffed up on both sides of the road, running for about a mile. Unplanted fields with irrigation trenches extended farther to the west. Cotton seemed almost bizarre to discover out here, yet cotton and Ethiopia shared a strange and fascinating history.

On a December day in 1951, as America was starting to work out plans to support Africa's postwar development, a noted Washington lawyer and former aide to President Harry Truman stepped into the office of the senior American diplomat for Africa and South Asia. This vast panorama of the world would spawn a parade of new nations exiting colonial rule by Britain and France. Yet in the early 1950s, that historic transition was a decade away. America the undisputed superpower after victory in world war was sorting out how it would exert influence over this sprawling area and its unfamiliar peoples.

While shrinking – India had won independence in 1947 – the British Empire still held much of Africa in its thrall. Even Ethiopia, while independent under Emperor Haile Selassie, was trying to restrain the administrative and military encroachment of its ally Britain, which had helped to expel the fascist Italian forces.

A tall, suave United States Navy officer turned White House insider, Clark Clifford had drafted Truman's landmark 1949 inaugural address known for "Point Four," which declared that

America would offer its vast resources to assist the impoverished stretches of the world. Without anyone realizing it at the time, this marked the opening chapter of overseas development aid – America's encounter with global poverty in exotic lands. With Africa losing its British accent, and America ascendant, the Emperor warmly embraced the initiative.

Truman's call for "making the benefits of our scientific advances and industrial progress available for the improvement and growth of underdeveloped areas" evolved into Kennedy's Foreign Assistance Act. Today that law confers the legal framework for America's health, education, agricultural, food relief, and democratic governance work with scores of partner governments in Africa, Asia, Latin America, and Eastern Europe.

Now back in private legal practice, Clifford had come to the State Department seeking introductions in Addis Ababa for an investment quest. "Cotton-raising, he thought, was intriguing because the Emperor now spends considerable sums of foreign exchange in importing cotton," recorded the official memorandum of Clifford's visit with the assistant secretary of state. "He mentioned the fertile lands of Ethiopia and the large supply of cheap labor."

Even as we journeyed through Omo fields, an American manufacturer of famous clothing brands was studying how it might source cotton from southern Ethiopia. The company had adopted an ambitious Africa manufacturing strategy and needed tens of thousands of acres to feed a future production line. Warily, the company eyed tracts of land offered in the Lower Omo Valley, where companies before them had discovered that far from being empty terrain for the taking, this land could ignite passions from the ground up. Deadly clashes had erupted between residents and foreign investment projects in the Omo and in the Gambella region to the north and west, including the palm-oil plantation of a Malaysian company. A Turkish manufacturer was wisely conducting a conflict assessment of the valley to avoid stumbling into the wrath of consumer activists in Europe, where its clothing was sold.

While the Lower Omo Valley has the uncanny ability to capture the attention of faraway outsiders, the river and its environs also exist in a great remoteness of confounding beauty. The river runs wild. The Omo in this stretch of the valley descending toward Lake Turkana wobbles and pivots like a drunk struggling to restore his relationship to gravity while careening down a street. As a satellite image reveals, the Omo coils and whirls repeatedly after exiting the Omo Kuraz sugarcane basin. At one point the river takes an abrupt left turn, then heads north for almost a mile, swings south and then westward, and loops north again before making a lazy turn and regaining its southward bearings toward Kenya.

A river obligated to fill a lake for 4 million years probably will go on a bender every so often.

Leaving our vehicles at the Omo's edge, we clambered down the steep, sandy riverbank to a cluster of dugout canoes and stepped gingerly into the rough-hewn vessels. The canoes motored across the dark flow, delivering us to the western shore. It was my first crossing of the Omo, which up to this point I had experienced only from its eastern banks. As we trudged up the embankment, the still, relentless heat of mid-day began to sap our energy. A white pickup truck from the local government office waited in the village above. We piled into the truck bed and gripped the sides as the vehicle bounced along a starkly beautiful plain unfolding for miles. Termite mounds pointed toward the broad sky. Flat, so flat this terrain, embellished by grass, thorn bushes over six feet high, dust.

A parley of mountains on the southern horizon in the direction of Kenya drew my gaze, a study in nature's geometry. One slope appeared to be a precise forty-five-degree line speared into the faraway landscape. As we drew closer to the river, earth tones gave way to green – a line of thick trees. The mind filled with dark green fronds of sugarcane caressed by dry breezes. We were about to discover that all this might be swallowed into the vast Omo Kuraz plantation pushing south from a distant wall of mountains. Swallowed and regurgitated as sugar.

Along the Omo River in this area resided the last pristine riverine forest in the drylands of sub-Saharan Africa, according to researchers. The Nyangatom and their forest rely on the swollen

Omo to spill over its banks, depositing rich soil for sorghum and maize, providing ample fish, and nourishing the trees. In turn, the forest offers wild plants, honey, and abundant wildlife for hunting.

Squeezed between the Omo and shrinking rangelands to the west due to drought and overgrazing, the Nyangatom people cling to a perilous existence. The western grasslands run into the Ilemi Triangle, a remote area northwest of Lake Turkana claimed by Kenya and South Sudan. In the Ilemi, large cattle herds have crowded out Nyangatom pastoralists trekking from the Omo lands of Ethiopia. And with the arrival of major agricultural development a new squeeze has gripped the landscape. The University of California, Berkeley, environmental scientist and policy researcher Claudia Carr lamented that her easy access to Nyangatom villagers had become exceptionally difficult due to "intense" surveillance by the Ethiopian Government and fears of punishment from local police. She recounted the shift in her book, *River Basin Development and Human Rights in Eastern Africa – A Policy Crossroads,* published three years after our visit.

We came upon over 200 tukuls in a traditional Nyangatom enclosure, yet few people – only a handful of elderly men and women. A health post, school, veterinary clinic, and other buildings scattered about revealed our find: the core of a future "villagization" settlement associated with the sugar plantation still unfolding far to the north. A woreda official said Chinese surveyors already were working in the area; the locals even knew where the sugar factories would be built. The government was talking to villages in the south near the Dassanech about moving to this villagization site, called Chungur.

Yet nothing was supposed to be happening here; we had figured that the huge footprint drawn on maps as a final phase to the far south would remain a planner's figment of the imagination. The sugar strategists had outsmarted us again. Here was proof that the plantation might be sprinting south out of its core far faster than we had dreamed. This was to be the final and biggest phase – as much as 100,000 hectares, or about a quarter-million acres. For scale, that's 10 times the land area of central Paris.

As we gathered ourselves for the journey back to Addis, a complex picture filled our collective thoughts. Thanks to a suspected insect bite, Oren nursed a swollen arm while she pondered the swirling issues of pastoralism, conflict, climate change, food security, and fighting poverty in the Horn of Africa. Brian, charmed by the locals, began to work on the idea of bringing Hamar women to the annual United Nations forum on Indigenous issues the following year.

Days before taking Brian, Oren, Walter and Leslie into the Omo, and thousands of miles away during a short visit to America, I had slipped into a dim restaurant along a street in Crystal City, an urban outpost across the Potomac River from Washington. While Crystal City neither sparkled nor dazzled, matters of consequence did unfold in quiet corners and offices.

The nucleus of the imagined city comprised office buildings for government agencies and weapons contractors situated close to the Pentagon, America's military headquarters. Nearby roared Ronald Reagan National Airport, where politicians and executives shuttled between marble and stone Washington avenues and glass and steel New York canyons.

Hotels, shops, and quick-service restaurants in Crystal City catered to the itinerant population, enablers of superpower America. For thousands of years, Indigenous peoples had hunted, fished, lived, and loved on this riverine land until the upstart American nation pushed them out and installed the seat of the fledgling American government, in 1790.

Eventually two individuals appeared at my table, the government relations chief and the lead Ethiopia researcher for one of the world's largest human rights groups. We engaged delicately; the great advocacy movement renowned for penning letters demanding freedom for political prisoners had not talked directly to the United States Government about Ethiopia in a long time. Nor could it set foot in Ethiopia.

Researchers tended to paint dark pictures devoid of illuminated openings to some better tomorrow. In my work, we needed options, or at least a roadmap toward a more palatable outcome, no matter how discouraging the overall picture. My goal was to relate some of the positive openings with the Ethiopians and to

The Omo flows through a great basin beneath the mountains of Omo National Park

steer the researchers toward the reality emerging in the Lower
Omo Valley. This was no longer about fending off the massive
development plans of the revolutionary democrats. The focus
had to turn toward helping the people adapt to the change surging
into their world like a wild Omo flood. While I don't recall using
the word survival, that's probably what I was thinking.

Our conversation shifted to the plight of the Oromo people in
Ethiopia, the largest ethnic group in the country yet paradoxically
bereft of political power. The Oromo speak a different language
than the highland Ethiopians of Amhara, rendered in a Latin script
that produces delightful words like *hooteela* for hotel. About half
of Oromos are Muslim in a predominantly Christian nation. And
Oromo traditional dress is more vibrant than one tends to find in

the devout Ethiopian heartland.

Ethiopia's Tigrayan-dominated ruling party viewed the Oromos as a threat, a rebellious wildfire at the doorstep of Addis Ababa. The coming national election heightened their paranoia. With journalists and dissidents locked up, intimidated, or sheltering outside the country, the ruling party wasn't winning any popularity contests. Meles might finally be staring at an end game, years after his demise.

The researcher had documented the intensifying repressive steps of the revolutionary democrats to counter and crush a perceived uprising across Oromia, which borders the lands of the Omo. A churning tide of protest rose when the government issued a master plan for Addis Ababa that called for expansion of the capital into Oromo territory to the south. Students marched at universities and sometimes were confronted by heavily armed security forces, bullets, arrests, and torture, according to more than 200 people interviewed for the human rights research. All manner of Oromos got caught up in the dragnet, from poets to pharmacists.

When an apolitical linguist and translator I knew got picked up by authorities and held at a prison notorious for torture, the crackdown transformed from testimonies in a report to a visceral reality. Upon his release, the good-natured linguist had fully absorbed the not-so-subtle language of blood and power, and he exited the country.

As the election approached and the government grew less tolerant of opponents, tension crackled across Ethiopia and space for opposition parties shrank to insignificance. Into this maelstrom came an American President on an official visit that was unofficially bizarre for almost ignoring the strife. Instead, Barack Obama put a positive spin on the future in the first address by a sitting American leader to the African Union in its Chinese-built assembly hall. Those stirring words of hope and liberation, however, failed to reverberate beyond those walls into the Ethiopian capital.

With the revolutionary democrats blocking dissenting voices from any meaningful role in the governance of the country, Ethiopia stood at a perilous moment, from Oromia to the Omo.

9

In the Minds of Men

IN THE SWEEP OF ETHIOPIA'S HISTORY, change sometimes crept in from afar and took long years to gain footing. So it was with the delicate issue of the minds of children in the Lower Omo Valley. A grand idea from the world beyond advanced silently toward that timeless terrain and its posterity.

The idea took form in London on a Friday afternoon in November 1945. Approaching a weekend of peace after six years of war, delegates from 44 countries, from Argentina to Yugoslavia, with the largest contingents from France, China, Britain, and the United States, took their seats. They met at the Institute of Civil Engineers, one of the few large buildings in London to escape German bombing raids.

An American delegate, Archibald MacLeish, a prominent poet and playwright who had fought in the First World War, set the tone for the bookish gathering at the opening session two weeks earlier. MacLeish urged conferees to increase the common understanding of the world's people as a path toward survival. "We must choose to live together, or we must choose, quite literally, not to live," he said.

Less than 10 weeks had passed since the surrender of the shattered Japanese Empire aboard an American battleship in Tokyo Bay. After the destruction of Hiroshima and Nagasaki by the searing flashes and apocalyptic thunder of American atomic bombs, militant Japan at last conceded, ending the Second World War. In moments, the dim hall of civil engineers in London once more would feel rumblings from that conflict.

A middle-aged woman rose from her seat on the dais, dressed in a dark suit, fashionably angular hat and a necklace draped in three strands. Ellen Wilkinson's appearance camouflaged years as an activist and British communist punctuated by a visit to the battlefronts of Spain's civil war in the 1930s. During the world war Wilkinson focused on the protection of civilians from air raids and in 1945 became Minister of Education under Prime Minister Clement Attlee. In that post she pushed through universal free secondary education as only the second woman to join a British cabinet. Upon her death in 1947 from heart failure, the wartime leader Winston Churchill said of her, "She had a very warm sympathy for social causes of all kinds and was fearless and vital in giving expression to them."

Tall windows flanked Wilkinson, revealing a gray stone city

emerging from years of grit and privation, scorched by episodes of violence. On the floor below, clerks and delegates shuffled papers as if nestled in a university library. In a sense they were. Wilkinson was poised to announce to the world the culmination of rumination and position-paper swapping, flowing largely from a French proposal shepherded by 73-year-old former Prime Minister Leon Blum, one of Europe's leading statesmen.

"The governments of the state parties to this constitution, on behalf of their peoples declare: that since wars begin in the minds of men, it is in the minds of men that the defenses of peace must be constructed," Wilkinson read in a crisp cadence as president of the conference. "That ignorance of each other's ways and lives has been a common cause throughout the history of mankind of that suspicion and mistrust between the peoples of the world through which their differences have, all too often, broken into war."

In reciting the preamble for a novel organization, Wilkinson expressed an intellectual stirring among war-battered peoples. During the decades to come the ideas that originated in London on that faraway Friday would seep into the Lower Omo Valley, crossing a chasm of deep time into the troubled minds of ancient men and women. Modern strivings for education plowed into an unknown that did not equal ignorance. Indigenous knowledge of life cycles, the environment, the cosmos, the passage and meaning of time, the relation of self to society, the moral debts within lived creation – was akin to the unexplored depths of the ocean. Not comprehending its richness, we could not imagine its value.

The first descriptive aspiration for this London-born offspring of an infant United Nations was "educational," followed by "scientific and cultural." From the 1950s most people would know the organization by a corporate acronym in vogue with the aloof internationalist glass-box skyscrapers of the era: UNESCO.

From the first possible moment, Ethiopia had signed up for the UN, chartered as a landmark political body for international security. It was a natural move for a country that had joined the peace-hugging League of Nations in 1923 after the First World War, one of four African members. Liberia, Egypt, and the Union of South Africa also took seats in the League, on a continent overrun by British, French, Belgian, and Portuguese colonial fabulists. Years later in the 1930s, Ethiopia's thin, erudite Emperor would expose the assembly as a paper lion while fascist fellow member Italy invaded, nerve-gassed and occupied dazed "Abyssinia."

After claiming a seat in the General Assembly of the United Nations, a country could choose whether to join the world body's multiplying agencies on labor, children's welfare, civil aviation, and the like. For long years Ethiopia hesitated on UNESCO, perhaps unsure of what value – or harm – this largely European crusade could bring to a land of noble peasants in the Horn of Africa. Technocrats searched for an answer. In 1955 UNESCO convened a conference of scholars on comparative education at the agency's institute in Hamburg.

"Owing to progressive technical development and to the overcoming of space and time, every nation has to a certain extent become the neighbor of all other nations – mentally," Professor Friedrich Schneider of Munich wrote in a paper that opened the meeting. The participants – 27 Europeans and one American – wondered how their research might apply to the cultures of Asia, South America – and Africa. Education "in every country is today more or less under the international and functional influence of foreign education," Schneider asserted. "This favorable – or it may be unfavorable – influence must not be left to chance but has to be watched and guided."

Years of lobbying by UNESCO's Paris-based culture-crats finally won over the government of Haile Selassie. A telegram arrived at UNESCO headquarters in May 1955, coincidentally a month after the Hamburg conference. Venerable, suspicious Ethiopia agreed to join the class with the shiny century's cool kids.

By the early 1970s, basic education had spread in Ethiopia, though vast areas in the highlands and the lowlands of this sheltered land remained without schools or teachers. Only one in six Ethiopian children attended primary school. Reaching higher grades proved even less likely. Just one in 20 Ethiopian youths ages 13 to 18 studied at a secondary school or vocational institute.

This narrow funnel for educated Ethiopians contributed to the country's status as one of the world's most impoverished societies.

To attack the problem, the imperial government conducted a groundbreaking study and recommended a rapid scale-up of primary education. What seemed like a logical move instead alarmed the Emperor's subjects. Many Ethiopians feared the proposed solution would bottle up their children in lower grades and hinder their path to higher education. Public opposition weakened an already creaking regime as a revolution simmered among activist university students and young military officers. History swiftly turned the page. A military junta toppled Haile Selassie in 1974, and the country slipped into a dark and bloody era. In schools, Marxist ideology infiltrated the curriculum. The regime embraced coercion and conformity, along with Castro's Cuba.

In the Lower Omo Valley under the declared communist regime that ruled until 1991, conformity delivered jarring change for the patriarchs of Hamar country: their girls were going into town for education. By the early years of the new century, the perception arose among Hamar men that the girls had fared poorly in town and fallen into either prostitution or forced marriages with highlanders. Eventually the friction grew beyond schooling as the land itself fell under the sway of a new political order. The men who one day would mold Molloka into the majordomo of the valley fanned out across the country to carry out policies promulgated from Addis Ababa.

Increasing government policing of conservation areas narrowed choices for the roaming Hamar and invited a sense of powerlessness. Accustomed to hunting for buffalos or lions in the wilds of the Omo Valley, the Hamar now regarded themselves as the prey of government interlopers. Labeling an Omo pastoralist who hunted in Mago National Park as a poacher struck many Hamar as strange and outlandish. Adjoining the northwestern frontier of Hamar territory, Mago shelters an immense array of mammals and birds across about 460,000 acres of riverine forests mixed with open and wooded grasslands. Who would choose to exile themselves from this promised land?

A mountain rises in the north of Mago to 8,250 feet, surely a feature that had impressed Hamar herders for centuries. Abundant water nourishes the flora and fauna of this remote landscape. Besides the Maki River, the Mago River flows through the center of the terrain, joining the Neri in a swamp. Conservationists count four of Africa's celebrated Big Five of the wild – buffalo, elephant, leopard, and lion – in the park, along with giraffes, cheetahs, and zebras. More than 200 types of birds flit through Mago, including the Egyptian plover, black-rumped waxbill, and dusky babbler.

In the schooling of their girls as in access to their traditional hunting lands, the Hamar began to feel the oppressive hand of a distant, invisible authority over which they had little to no control and even less influence. That remote power answered to some other force, imposed rules alien to their mindscape, and above all, in the view of the Hamar, just didn't listen.

As so often happened in the Omo Valley, the trouble began in darkness. A team from the Hamar Woreda, or district, administration had gone to the village of Worro to determine how to take into custody Hamar hunters accused of killing scouts and poaching wild animals in Mago. The authorities also wanted to discuss the education of girls in the communities.

It was the middle of January in 2015, the Millennium Development year, a time of fair and dry weather in Ethiopia and a buoyant mood following the celebration of Christmas in the Orthodox calendar. In the highlands far to the north, Orthodox Christians would gather in a few days for the festival of Timkat marking the baptism of Jesus in the River Jordan. Crowds clad in snowy white cloaks would collect around a pool in Gondar and in an immense field and horse racing course in Addis Ababa. Orthodox priests draped in lavish robes and toting elegant, fringed parasols and intricate silver crosses would thread through the faithful offering blessings.

While jubilant, the country also braced for a surreal political season. In four months, the ruling revolutionary democrats would attempt to affirm their version of popular rule at the ballot box. Revolution had long since slipped away, leaving only stubborn pride, spiteful reaction, and a disciplined devotion to constitutional procedure. Tension surged in the country amid protests by the Oromo people and the resistance of the ruling party to open campaigning by opposition candidates. The revolutionary democrats had adopted the mentality and methods of a siege, in what would turn out to be their historic miscalculation.

Ethiopia had entered a period of far-reaching transformation that would thrust the country fully into the new century. Yet at the time few could see this. Tensions also were rising in Hamar country. Because the Hamar in one village had severely beaten the chief administrator and other officials of the district during discussions a short time before, this contingent of district officials arrived with a police escort. The police toted Kalashnikovs and at least one machine gun.

Hamar residents from five kebeles, as Ethiopia calls village-level communities, already were adamant that the so-called poachers would not fall into the hands of the police. The government didn't feed the animals of Mago, didn't water these wild beasts, or provide medicine, so why did hunting in the park concern the authorities?

Outside the town of Dimeka, the police test-fired an aging machine gun. In one account, this was done merely to ensure that the weapon still functioned. Hearing the discharge, the Hamar residents of Worro assumed the police had in mind more than rounding up poachers, according to a mediator later sent to the area. Perhaps they had come to disarm the community. That fear had long unsettled the Hamar living in this part of the woreda. Three years earlier they had refused to register their rifles with the government.

The police chose to shelter for the night in a primary school and sent elders into town to announce a meeting with the community for the next day. The visitors soon discovered that the Hamar in Worro were in no mood for talking. Townsfolk chased away the elders and shouted them down as enemies, according to a policeman in the group. As darkness fell, a woman rushed up to the school and warned the visitors that they were surrounded by armed men from the village. Run, she urged. Outside, the policemen heard war songs and the firing of rifles. The district officials insisted on continuing with their mission and stayed put, prepared for a fitful night.

The next morning, as the police went out to collect water from a nearby river, young Hamar men fired on them, the police officer recalled. A shootout ensued. Two policemen were killed and four seriously wounded. The Hamar had drawn blood and the ire of the Ethiopian state.

On the north side of the valley in Jinka, the administrative capital, Molloka stepped from his car on the way into his office and found the zonal security chief waiting to brief him on the outbreak of violence. The clash caught Molloka by surprise; the woreda officials had gone to the area without his knowledge amid an effort at Molloka's level to confer with Hamar elders on the tense issues with the government. As the situation had turned deadly and remained volatile, Molloka recommended to the regional state authorities that a special security force be sent immediately to the scene.

Several hours later the special force members arrived in Worro and found themselves quickly encircled by the Hamar militants. Another gunfight erupted during the afternoon. In the fusillade of bullets, four more policemen and a female teacher were killed. A Hamar resident also died, according to a mediator. The special force managed to free the pinned-down officials, and at night the survivors left the dead and escaped to nearby Dimeka. In Jinka, an emergency security committee that included regional officials convened under Molloka's leadership. Concerned about the fate of Dimeka, the group recommended that federal police and Ethiopian defense forces deploy to the town to impose order.

The Hamar War of 2015 startled the authorities from Jinka up to Addis Ababa. The Hamar had not clashed with the government in such deadly fashion in more than 60 years, dating back to the Assile War of 1948 that had ensnared the Emperor's security forces in a dispute over cattle raiding.

A week after the conflict, the situation had calmed enough for Molloka to make the journey to Dimeka for talks with Hamar elders. He returned several times, eventually opening the way for the Hamar to return to the food markets of Dimeka and for a semblance of public services including health care to resume.

Molloka's own health began to falter as the stress of the conflict began to take a toll. Feeling ill during one discussion, he sought painkillers at a health clinic. Saddened by the deadly violence in Hamar country, Molloka would later describe this period as "the worst time of my leadership."

With the support of regional and national officials, Molloka turned to Awoke Aike, himself of Hamar origin, to try to calm the conflict and deepen dialogue on the root issues of the war. A tall member of the national parliament with a kindly face, Ato Awoke was one of the few people who could cope in both worlds. Perhaps he could restore a measure of long-term peace. The terrain and people he knew well, from long days past. Awoke was born to a chief in Hamar country in 1956. At age 12 he left his kebele and ventured less than 10 miles to Dimeka for primary school, then shifted to Jinka for high school. His father envisioned him as a future leader in the Omo Valley. College followed, with Awoke earning a degree in veterinary science.

Awoke returned to his homeland to work as an animal doctor in Turmi, on the southern edge of Hamar territory. With the collapse of the communist regime in Addis Ababa, local rule came to the Omo Valley. Awoke's father encouraged, even pushed him, to get into politics. The reluctant son, more enamored of working with animals than joining self-styled revolutionary politicians, bowed to his father's wishes.

In the emerging Ethiopia of Meles, Awoke climbed fast. His

first post was agricultural department head in Hamar Woreda. Next came election to the regional state parliament. By 2000 Awoke had advanced to South Omo Zone administrator, becoming one of Molloka's predecessors. Addis Ababa beckoned five years later as Awoke was elected to the national House of Peoples' Representatives. He would spend a decade there as the Meles regime consolidated its power along with development wins and cozy ties with American philanthropists and Chinese banks. In the assembly, Awoke served as deputy chief of the permanent committee on pastoralists.

When Awoke reached Dimeka three days after the fighting he found a dire situation – for the highlanders and for the Hamar themselves. Civil servants including teachers, health workers, and agricultural advisers had fled. Angry Hamar residents had descended on the symbols of the hated regime in Addis Ababa and wrecked schools, health clinics, and government bureaus. The people of these troubled Hamar lands were in trouble, too, with social services gone and the town and its markets off limits.

Awoke went to work. He identified the leader of the revolt and tracked down his telephone number. During a call Awoke negotiated the release of the bodies of slain police officers and the return of their weapons. The rebels agreed to halt the conflict, and the situation stabilized to the point that Awoke returned to his parliamentary duties. However, the war merely had paused. Although Ethiopian security forces were of sufficient strength in the aftermath of the initial fighting to go after the Hamar assailants, officials including Molloka concluded that such an operation likely would result in unacceptable casualties.

Four months later, the police moved in on the suspected head of the rebellion and arrested him in an attempt to force the surrenders of others involved in the January attack. A Hamar elder says the individual was a "nobleman," a spiritual leader who had blessed the Hamar war plan. While he did not directly ignite the war, he supported the conflict carried out by the Hamar people. In the elder's telling, they went to war together.

The arrested leader passed a message to his Hamar supporters to rise up. As if waiting for this moment, they responded en masse. Hamar residents streamed in from their villages to Dimeka and surrounded the town, threatening deadly violence against residents. This time the government mounted a more intimidating response to quell the rebellion. Soldiers blocked roads leading out of town. The Hamar responded by cutting down trees to hinder access to roads leading to their villages.

Raising the stakes, the Ethiopian army arrived to support the regional special force. Both sides exchanged gunfire for days. Reports at the time talked of scores of deaths and wounded soldiers flown to Addis Ababa. A spot report at the time indicated that a businessman and a member of the zonal special force were killed in clashes with the Hamar. To this day, the exact number of casualties in the second phase of the conflict remains unknown.

If there is an official report on the clashes that would shed light on the toll, that account is concealed in the deep recesses of the Ethiopian state. At least two soldiers were wounded, according to Awoke.

On the fourth day of the fighting, the army moved in heavy weapons and fired over the Hamar gathered around Dimeka, trying to disperse them. Awoke insists the army discharged only warning shots and didn't aim at the Hamar with these more lethal guns. He says the rebels eventually ended their siege and drifted back to their villages.

In the wake of the violent standoff, Awoke undertook an intense round of talks with the Hamar community, holding as many as five meetings a week to discuss grievances and the government's response. He acknowledged that the government's handling of the poaching and the education of Hamar girls was heavy-handed and would change. For the Hamar, letting a girl go off to school in a town over the horizon amounted to a loss of wealth as well as culture. A future dowry, of honey, cattle, goats, and other perquisites disappeared along with the girl, according to an elder.

Awoke and his mediation team pledged that the government wouldn't force the Hamar to send their girls to schools off their lands without the permission of parents. Yet the team explained that the government viewed the education of girls as a right, and the Hamar needed to reconcile its stance with that policy.

The United Nations Declaration on the Rights of Indigenous Peoples adopted eight years earlier had touched on this issue, attempting to balance the interests of governments and their original populations, though perhaps muddling the message.

In Article 14, the declaration states that "indigenous people have the right to establish and control their educational systems" in a way "appropriate to their cultural methods of teaching and learning." The declaration further asserts that Indigenous children "have the right to all levels and forms of education of the State without discrimination."

Even as efforts at reconciliation pressed ahead, anger still flowed through Hamar country and almost cost Awoke his life. One day he was traveling to Lala village about 20 miles from Dimeka, accompanied by the security chief for the Hamar Woreda and the security head for the entire South Omo Zone, along with the deputy administrator of the zone. On the way the team came upon an angry crowd that stopped their car and forced them out. They were taken to a nearby school and detained in a swirl of threats.

The armed mob shouted that the men were plotting with "Amharas" – outsiders or highlanders – to kill Hamar people. The leader of the ambush pointed at Awoke and said he has caused us no problem. He turned to the security chiefs and said they should be killed. The zonal security chief they accused of cruelty toward their community, taking their girls to school in Jinka, the zonal capital, and allowing them to fall into adultery, abandoning Hamar culture and marrying "Amharas."

Someone pointed a gun at the security chief's stomach and threatened to shoot. Awoke recalls that he managed to stay calm and tried to defuse the confrontation, sensing that intimidation rather than deadly violence was the mob's intent. In a polite tone, Awoke asked for forgiveness and apologized for the use of force. Elders arrived on the scene to calm the situation. The tension lifted, and eventually the team was freed.

"We all survived because we all are originally from well-known families in the Hamar area," Awoke recalls. "But if Amharas had been with us, they would have killed them."

In the ensuing months, as anger eased, health centers and water points were repaired and reopened. In September the government and the Hamar held a peace conference in a show of reconciliation. On the surface, at least, the conflict had ceased.

Years later, reconciliation seems to be a work in progress. A Hamar elder says his people remain at odds with modern Ethiopia: "Full peace has not come."

Epilogue

IN THE DINGY PORT AREA of Rio de Janeiro, Brazilian artist Eduardo Kobra had to tilt his eyes up, and far to the right and left, to size up his canvas: a warehouse wall running more than 600 feet in length and rising to the height of a four-story building. As if the surface area confronting Kobra wasn't daunting enough, the ambition for this Olympian work loomed even larger: to create a signature art piece for the world's biggest sports competition.

During the next two months, after emptying hundreds of swirling gallons of paint and thousands of hissing spray-paint cans onto the vast brick surface, Kobra's mural "Ethnicities" emerged, a gift for Brazil. With his characteristic overlay of neon geometry, Kobra had rendered glowing portraits of five Indigenous people representing humanity.

The portrait at the far left, chosen to capture Africa, shows a woman with clusters of rings dangling from a headdress framing both sides of her proud visage. A yellow horizontal line streaks across her nose and reappears among four other tribal figures arrayed along the wall from Brazil, Siberia, Thailand, and New Guinea. Diagonal stripes of red, blue, green, purple, and orange glide across the woman's lips and cheeks.

From a billion Africans, Kobra had chosen for his iconic mural a Mursi woman from the Omo Valley.

"It's a mural that speaks of the coming together of all the world's people," Kobra told the Spanish news agency EFE. "It justly speaks of the importance of leaving aside religious and political differences, of avoiding conflicts and really finding the union of all people."

Not long after the Rio Games, filmmakers from Hollywood appeared in the Omo Valley. The production designer and her associates were journeying across Africa, seeking artistic inspiration for a groundbreaking movie. The film would startle audiences by portraying a technologically advanced, culturally rich, and supremely confident civilization thriving in the heart of Africa. With a mesmerizing cinematic canvas, *Black Panther* wiped away stereotypes while suffusing the screen with a gleaming, inspiring vision. The symbolism of a defiant, independent African domain with great wardrobe choices reminded some people of Ethiopia – minus the sleek technology.

In their own valley homeland, the Mursi, Bodi, Hamar, and other peoples still struggled to preserve their identities, grazing lands, and mystifying customs as the world year by year pressed in. On a planet addicted to mass and social media, instant pundits, and ceaseless preening, the humble Omo peoples attained the status of celebrities, elevated as cultural survivors. Awestruck visitors to the valley still aimed their lenses at these captivating people, sending those images onto millions of screens around the world.

On rare occasion, emissaries from the Omo slipped into that other world to tell their stories. During the same months that Hamar communities were waging war with the Ethiopian government, two daring women from another part of Hamar territory set foot in the American state of Minnesota on a trip sponsored by their American benefactor. Gulo and Dobi marveled at the trappings of another planet, a sensory overload of astonishing gizmos, bustle – and people. They wondered what sort of Creator could be responsible for all of this, so unlike their realm back home.

On a brisk spring day, a crowd of middle-aged, middle-class, and mostly white women and men packed a meeting hall at the Rotary Club in Duluth to hear from the Hamar visitors. The Minnesotans had supported literacy programs, water wells, and orphans in Hamar country, while achieving something much more profound and surprising, even to the Hamar. The women from afar had punctured the gender bubble and gained a respected voice in the affairs of their male-dominated community.

Dobi stood to the side of the podium, wearing her traditional goat skin and cowrie shells layered onto a modern, blue fleece jacket, watching as Gulo spoke into a microphone, her full cheeks drawing back a smile. Later Dobi reflected on her mind-bending trip. "Before I met you, I only felt responsible for my family and community," she said through an interpreter at another gathering of Minnesota supporters. "Now I realize that you also are my community, and I return home holding your well-being in my thoughts and in my heart."

Ever so slowly the world is waking to the voice, value, and resonance of Indigenous peoples. A century ago, the world's governments shunned the first peoples; the League of Nations rejected their request to address the body in 1923. Only in the first decade of the following century did the League's successor, the United Nations, usher Indigenous priorities into the spotlight. Adopted with the support of 143 countries, the United Nations Declaration on the Rights of Indigenous Peoples initially was opposed by the United States. Barack Obama reversed that decision as he expanded dialogue with Native Americans. In a statement, the United States asserted that the declaration "has both moral and political force." Yet little happened in the next decade to bring the document to life.

In 2021, the American Bar Association, the powerful voice of lawyers in the United States, adopted a resolution asking all levels of American government to "endorse and implement" the world body's landmark stance. The group urged the United States Congress to enact a law that would require America to bring its laws into alignment with the declaration.

"By the terms of the UN Charter, General Assembly resolutions are generally 'recommendatory' rather than 'binding' in nature," the lawyers explained. "Yet, sometimes, the provisions of Declarations are so widely accepted that they come to embody 'customary international' or 'general principles' of international law. The Universal Declaration on Human Rights of 1948 is one example. The Declaration on the Rights of Indigenous Peoples is starting to move in this direction."

The American Bar highlighted the declaration's concept of "free, prior and informed consent" of Indigenous peoples before actions are taken that may affect their land, natural resources, or well-being. This principle had animated our years of monitoring across the Lower Omo Valley.

California, frequently a global pacesetter in causes social and political, had pivoted toward the issue even before the American lawyers delivered their argument. California's governor signed an executive order that committed the most populous American state to use tribal knowledge of ecology in conservation and land management.

In the years after his visit to the Omo Valley, Brian pressed ahead against bureaucratic inertia and political resistance to align American development strategy and investments with the rising sensitivity to Indigenous rights, especially around land use. In a statement marking the International Day of the World's

Indigenous Peoples, 9 August, Brian noted that national education curricula were starting to integrate Indigenous knowledge and that public health policies had begun to adopt traditional learning. Welcome steps, though too often achieved only on paper.

"Despite progress that has been made in implementing the Declaration," Brian observed, "there continues to be a gap between formal recognition of indigenous peoples and implementation of policies on the ground."

In 2020, Brian's persistence paid off. The United States Agency for International Development, the world's largest poverty-fighting operation, adopted a policy on promoting Indigenous rights. The head of the agency praised Indigenous communities for defending their lands and cultures "from competing demands on resources." The policy described collaboration as a "practical and moral imperative." Effective engagement with these resilient stewards would help advance democracy, human rights, citizen-responsive governance, and sustainable prosperity.

Outside America, action also stirred. After organizing a special meeting of the General Assembly known as the World Conference on Indigenous Peoples, the United Nations began to look more deeply into how to bring Indigenous views and expertise into its deliberations. In some venues this was happening, such as UNESCO, the International Fund for Agricultural Development, and the long-winded Intergovernmental Committee on Intellectual Property and Genetic Resources,

Traditional Knowledge and Folklore.

In other arenas of global consequence, the role of first peoples cried out for a higher profile. As super-storms, persistent droughts and slushy glaciers multiplied, the prominence of the United Nations Framework Convention on Climate Change – a name so bland as to obscure one of mankind's most urgent worries - grew in the popular mind. Perhaps the scientists were right that a crisis over excessive carbon dioxide and methane in the atmosphere would not end well unless broadly confronted – a green world war. Yet governments struggled to shape a united front able to cool off the planet before Earth's climate machine turned its full wrath on humanity.

Titanic battles loomed between the fossil fuel legacy industries, still choking the skies of rising countries like India, and the clean-energy evangelists calling on the worship of sun, wind, and water. Who better to offer solutions than humans in places like drylands Africa who had weathered climate cycles for millennia? Who better to preserve the forests soaking up rogue carbon than the people who live among the trees and respect their rustling majesty? Who better to teach us how to cope with the worst effects of a warming planet than those who strive for a balance between the needs of man and nature?

Ironically Ethiopia was emerging as an African green superpower even while scrambling the future of the Lower Omo Valley. The abrupt arrival of a new leader heralded an even more rapid shift into this era. In wresting power from the Tigrayan cabal, a shrewd former cybersecurity official in the ruling party's ranks named Abiy Ahmed yanked Ethiopia into a more confident concept of itself. The youthful Abiy, youngest African leader at the time, could relate to Ethiopia's hordes of restless young people. Abiy hailed from the majority Oromo community and thus put the stamp of representative rule on his legitimacy. And Abiy swiftly communicated that the environment and green energy would feature in his plans.

A photograph taken in the exuberant early days of his government shows Abiy in shirt and tie bent to the task of planting a tree without sullying his suit pants. His Green Legacy Initiative set a target of 20 billion seedlings to be planted in about five years. (Ensuring that those seedlings would grow into viable trees would require every Ethiopian to look after a small forest of almost 200 plantings.)

To supply Ethiopia's growing population and industries, Abiy's government announced plans to build dozens of renewable energy projects, from solar to wind and geothermal. With Kenya's help, Ethiopia was beginning to tap the fiery steam of Mother Earth so rich along the Great Rift Valley. The Corbetti Caldera, an ancient volcanic crater venting puffs of steam south of Addis Ababa, beckoned as a great new source of cheap electricity for a people eager to show off their power.

Abiy oversaw the completion of the Grand Ethiopian

Renaissance Dam on the Nile and thus the fulfillment of downstream Egypt's nightmare. As a great reservoir lifted into the terrain of northwestern Ethiopia behind the dam, water became a de facto source of international confrontation in Africa. On the Omo River, the Gibe III dam, Africa's tallest, began to generate electricity as thunderous tubes of water shot out from its spillways into the canyon below. A cyan-hued reservoir covering more than 80 square miles pressed into the towering white concrete wall. Below the precipice a milky brown ribbon of river ran south toward the Omo Valley ancients, though perhaps too diminished to sustain flood-retreat agriculture. Yet for sheer visual drama there were few sights in manmade Africa to rival the spectacle that Meles dreamed, and his successors built.

Downstream, the Sugar Corp's sprawling project lurched forward, with fresh scrutiny. UNESCO's World Heritage Committee, concerned by the scale of the Omo Kuraz sugarcane footprint, requested a report from the Ethiopian Government "as a matter of urgency" on the relocation of pastoralists and the possible effects on human origins sites in the vicinity. The committee wondered about the progress of a European Union-funded effort to preserve paleontological sites.

Ethiopia responded in early 2018, describing the reduced scale of the sugar project from the initial concept, and pledging to protect the ancient sites located near the southern extent of the plan, rich in fossils and tools dating back 2.5 million years. The

Ethiopian planners had cut the size of the sugarcane cultivation area to 100,000 hectares from 175,000 hectares – a reduction to roughly 250,000 acres from around 430,000 – after "seeing the productive nature of the project area." Nyangatom lands would be spared from sacrificing those 75,000 hectares to sugarcane. As a result, the number of sugar factories would be reduced to four from five, still capable of producing 1.3 million tons of sugar each year.

Meanwhile, the peoples of the Lower Omo Valley seemed delighted, after visiting the original Wonji Shoa Sugar Factory, opened in 1954, according to Sugar Corp. An era of good feelings swept southward into the Omo Valley, the company proclaimed. Experience-sharing programs had "brought about [an] attitudinal shift from the locals so that they became more eager to see the factory under construction at their place start producing sugar."

UNESCO told Ethiopia that it had not answered crucial questions: on the boundary area for the development sites, environmental and social impacts, the degree of community consultations, effects on the Lake Turkana basin, and the state of conservation. Questions always outnumbered answers in the Lower Omo Valley.

A few months after he took over as prime minister, Abiy traveled to the Omo Valley to open Omo Kuraz Sugar Factory Three, built by a Chinese company with Chinese financing to cover the cost of 8 billion Ethiopian birr. At full production capacity, the factory could turn out up to 1,000 tons of raw or refined sugar each day. A year earlier, Sugar Factory Two had opened, capable of crushing 12,000 tons of sugarcane daily for both sugar and ethanol. The plant also could generate excess electricity for the national grid. To its timeless accolades of human ingenuity, the Omo Valley could add yet another: the hardest-working sugarcane on the planet.

One afternoon a voice, clear and familiar, issues from my phone. The English is smoother than I remember. The tone friendly and somewhat reflective. Seven years after I last saw him, Molloka and I are talking again.

"Why don't you come to Addis? Are you afraid of me?" he jokes.

The intervening years had hurled political triumphs and personal challenges toward the boy whom fate had elevated from his Maale homeland. In the election of 2015, he attained a prestigious role in national affairs. Elected as a member of parliament representing his home turf, Molloka served on the committee overseeing the national budget and expenditures. The youthful interpreter for Ethiopia's development revolutionaries had ascended from his Indigenous community in the Lower Omo Valley to the height of Ethiopian power. Yet shortly after, failing kidneys sent him to India for transplants followed by two years of recuperation. Once his health improved, Molloka attended the Meles Zenawi Academy for new legislators and there met the future prime minister Abiy during a month of training sessions.

Molloka still endorses what he calls the transformational changes brought about by Meles. "The development revolution is deeply rooted in Ethiopia," he says. Yet the idea of villagization – gathering scattered pastoralists – has fizzled out. The ambitions of the Omo Kuraz planners, to push sugarcane far to the south, have not materialized. For Molloka one goal remains elusive yet essential: to bring the ancients of the Omo Valley into the modern world. He describes himself as "aggressive" when faced with this problem.

"The main strategy for changing the people is education," Molloka says. "There is no education there, they are in a thousand years not trained and not educated. They continue their traditional way of life. So, the government wants to change their life for the better lifestyle. At the time I accepted fully that plan, which is beneficial and useful for pastoralists."

The fault lines of our encounters years ago remained, pressures yet to be released in this valley beyond all valleys, in this homeland of humanity.

"Today you ask me how the culture of the Mursi and Bodi will continue," Molloka notes as our pleasant two-hour conversation encounters familiar frictions. "The issue for me is the pastoralists are not benefiting as human beings, no clean water supply, no health, no food security."

"I want to change their lifestyles, but you are always asking about the culture. Why?"

Notes and Acknowledgements

DURING MY YEARS IN ETHIOPIA, and especially in my work in the Lower Omo Valley, I benefited from the support and wisdom of an exceptional group of colleagues including Dennis Weller, Trevor Hublin, Carol Wilson, Brian Gilchrest, Endegena Ashenafi, Peter Heaney, Patrick Wegner, David Mogollon, Bizuwork Ketete, Thomas Huyghebaert, then-deputy chief of mission Molly Phee, Ambassador Patricia Haslach, Brian Keane, Gary Linden, Jason Fraser, Lori Pappas, John Graham, and Awetu Simesso. While their influence shaped what I accomplished and has informed this book, the responsibility for the words on these pages and any flaws therein rests with the author.

Nancy Aluoch Oluoch, for your loving support I am so grateful.

Ethiopian researcher Asnake Samuel provided invaluable assistance in reconstructing the Hamar War of 2015 and its aftermath by finding key participants for interviews. I am grateful as well for his efforts to locate Ato Molloka for a conversation that helped bring this story of the Lower Omo Valley of Ethiopia up to the present.

Chapter 1

These tools are "evidence of the oldest known technical activities of prehistoric beings": "Lower Valley of the Omo" in World Heritage List of the United Nations Educational, Scientific and Cultural Organization.

Two valuable general histories of Ethiopia are: Paul B. Henze, *Layers of Time* and Bahru Zewde, *A History of Modern Ethiopia, 1855-1991*.

Chapter 2

Speech by Prime Minister Meles Zenawi for 13th Annual Pastoralists Day celebrations in Jinka, South Omo Zone, on 25 January 2011.

Ethiopia's victors, the tenacious Tigrayan guerrilla band: For an in-depth look at the tumultuous revolutionary period following the toppling of Emperor Haile Selassie in 1974, see: Gebru Tareke, *The Ethiopian Revolution: War in the Horn of Africa*.

A political scientist once observed that this carnival-tent title: The British academic Christopher Clapham suggested this to me over dinner. Clapham has written important books on Ethiopian and regional politics including *Transformation and Continuity in Revolutionary Ethiopia* (1988), *The Horn of Africa: State Formation and Survival* (2017), *Third World Politics: An Introduction* (1985), and *African Guerrillas* (1998).

Ethiopia's plans "accompany an aggressive resettlement program targeting the local populations": Oakland Institute, "Understanding Land Investment Deals in Africa: Ignoring Abuse in Ethiopia, DFID and USAID in the Lower Omo Valley" (July 2013).

Chapter 3

In early 1949, American diplomats pondered how to deliver the news to an ally: "Memorandum of Conversation, by the Acting Secretary of State," 11 January 1949, in *Foreign Relations of the United States, 1949, the Far East and Australasia*, Volume VII, Part 1.

"The seizure of power was not on the agenda; Bandung was not concerned with how to take power": Richard Wright, *The Color Curtain,* in *Black Power: Three Books From Exile*.

On 12 June 1951, the Imperial Ethiopian Government granted HVA a lease: Imperial Ethiopian Government, Ministry of Commerce and Industry, letter to the Assistant to the Director of Point Four, Addis Ababa, 19 September 1952. In *National Archives of the United States*, RG 469, USOM to Ethiopia, 1951-1952.

Cane would crowd more than 300,000 acres: The Omo Kuraz sugar plantation was designed to expand in phases, from north to south along the Omo River, as shown in maps provided by the Ethiopian Sugar Corporation and reproduced in Government of Ethiopia reports.

Ethiopian Investment Agency, "Investment Opportunity Profile for Sugarcane Plantation and Processing in Ethiopia" (June 2012).

World demand grows about 1.4 percent a year: Organization for Economic Cooperation and Development and Food and Agriculture Organization of the United Nations, *OECD-FAO Agricultural Outlook, 2020-2029,* Section 5, Sugar, 9.

For a valuable study of the Omo sugarcane development, villagization, and the effects on the Indigenous pastoralists, see: Yidneckachew Ayele Zikargie and Logan Cochrane, "Modernist Land Development-Induced Villagisation: Deconstructing Socio-Economic Rights of Pastoralists in South Omo, Ethiopia," *Forum for Development Studies,* (June 2022).

Chapter 4

Ivo Strecker and Jean Lydall, editors, *The Perils of Face: Essays on Cultural Contact, Respect and Self-Esteem in Southern Ethiopia.*

"'What counts is the barjo of the people": Ivo Strecker, "'Face' as a Metaphor of Respect and Self-Esteem. Lessons From Hamar" in *The Perils of Face, 89.*

Lydall followed *The Women Who Smile* (1990) with *Two Girls Go Hunting* (1991), *Our Way of Loving* (1994), and *Duka's Dilemma*

(2001).

Jean delves into beating rituals: Jean Lydall, "Beating Around the Bush," *Proceedings of the Eleventh International Conference of Ethiopian Studies, Volume II* (1994).

"A girl who gets whipped": Lydall, "Beating Around the Bush," 6.

European Union Trust Fund for Stability, "Cross-Border Analysis and Mapping, Cluster 1: Southwest Ethiopia-Northwest Kenya," (August 2016), 13-14.

Jean's films achieved an astonishing level of intimacy: Frederic Gesing, "Interview with Jean Lydall" (April 2012), video published by Arcadiafilm at https://www.youtube.com/watch?v=L1bzxBO6cFE

"But the memory of the Amhara conquest has been incorporated into their patriarchal ideology": Yukio Miyawaki, "Hor Memory of Sidaama Conquest" in *The Perils of Face,* 185-206.

The Maale elite had become "Ethiopian landlords": Donald L. Donham, *Work and Power in Maale, Ethiopia,* 50.

The new Maale king Bailo ... removed his regal necklace: Donham, *Work and Power in Maale, Ethiopia*, 50.

"Exotic representations" of Mursi women: Shauna LaTosky, "Images of Mursi Women and the Realities They Reveal and Conceal," in Felix Girke, editor, *Ethiopian Images of Self and Other,* 121-145.

Chapter 5

It wasn't just the Ethiopian Spice Girls stirring up trouble: The British Government ended funding to the Yegna project in 2017, following a review.

The Mursi … meticulously managed grazing and cultivation areas: Shauna LaTosky and Olisarali Olibui, "Pastoralists Do Plan! Experiences of Mursi Land Use Planning, South Omo, Ethiopia," *Making Rangelands Secure*, Bulletin No. 6 (August 2015).

Chapter 6

When rains faltered in these lands, the two peoples sometimes clashed: Yntiso Gebre, "Environmental Change, Food Crises and Violence in Dassanech, Southern Ethiopia" (2012), 10.

Activists in America kept up the heat: Oakland Institute, "Ignoring Abuse in Ethiopia," 11.

Coercion carried deadly consequences: Tareke, *The Ethiopian Revolution, 150.*

Chapter 7

The British Government would twice reject freedom of information requests to release our report: John Vidal, "EU Diplomats Reveal Devastating Impact of Ethiopia Dam Project on Remote Tribes," *Guardian*, 3 September 2015.

A few years earlier, an aerial and ground survey of Omo

National Park: African Parks Ethiopia, "Omo National Park Report for the Wet Season Aerial Survey," (2007).

Integral to Suri culture … is a sort of devotion to violence: Jon Abbink, "Restoring the Balance: Violence and Culture Among the Suri of Southern Ethiopia," 82-84, in Goran Aijmer and Jon Abbink, editors, *Meanings of Violence: A Cross-Cultural Perspective.*

The poetry-writing tycoon opened his land to public use: Paul Van Vlissingen, Obituary, *Independent,* 26 August 2006.

As we investigated this area, the editors of the Journal of Human Evolution were preparing an article: Michelle S.M. Drapeau et al, "The Omo Mursi Formation: A Window Into the East African Pliocene," *Journal of Human Evolution* (October 2014), 64-79.

The major fossil sites and findings along the Omo River near Lake Turkana are described in in the Government of Ethiopia's report to the director of UNESCO's World Heritage Center, "State Party Report on the State of Conservation of the Lower Omo Valley of Ethiopia" submitted on 28 January 2014, and "Progress Report on the State of Conservation of the Lower Omo Valley Heritage Property," submitted on 30 January 2018, and in Yonas Beyene, "Ethiopia's Paleoanthropological World Heritage Sites: Research and Conservation," part of a UNESCO report, *Human Origin Sites and the World Heritage Convention in Africa* (2012).

This landmark discovery owed much to Johanson's first

African fieldwork: Johanson recalls his arrival in the Omo Valley and his later discovery of Lucy in northern Ethiopia in Chapter 1, "The Woman Who Shook Up Man's Family Tree" in *Lucy's Legacy: The Quest for Human Origins,* written with Kate Wong.

"Today Ethiopia celebrates the fact that the proportion of people below the poverty line has been halved": Ethiopia National Planning Commission and the United Nations in Ethiopia, "Assessment of Ethiopia's Progress Toward the MDGs" (October 2015).

Chapter 8

The policy laid out four objectives: United States Agency for International Development. "Policy on Promoting the Rights of Indigenous Peoples" (March 2020).

A cascade of livelihood "shocks" jarred the pastoral scene: "USAID Pastoralist Areas Resilience Improvement and Market Expansion (PRIME) Project Impact Evaluation: Endline Survey Report," (September 2019), 22-38.

Researchers looked at 20 factors that together measured "resilience": "PRIME Impact Evaluation," 61-92.

"Cotton-raising, he thought, was intriguing": "Mr. Clark Clifford's Interest in Ethiopia," Memorandum of Conversation, 4 December 1951. In *National Archives of the United States*, RG 59, Office Files of Assistant Secretary of State McGhee, 1945-1953, folder "Ethiopia 1948 – Memoranda."

The researcher had documented the intensifying repressive steps of the revolutionary democrats to counter and crush a perceived uprising: Amnesty International, "Because I Am Oromo: Sweeping Repression in the Oromia Region of Ethiopia," (2014).

Chapter 9

The idea took form in London: *Conference for the Establishment of the United Nations Educational, Scientific and Cultural Organization,* 1-16 November 1945, is a detailed report on the proceedings, including transcribed comments by the American delegate MacLeish and others. A video of Wilkinson giving remarks introducing UNESCO is found at: *https://www.unesco.org/archives/multimedia/document-15*

Technocrats searched for an answer: Friedrich Schneider, "The Conception of Comparative Education" in "Comparative Education: An International Meeting Held From 12-16 April 1955, at the UNESCO Institute for Education, Hamburg," 10.

The Ethiopia telegram is cited in Marie Huber, "Ethiopia and UNESCO: Strategic Cooperation in the Global Sixties," shared under Creative Commons Attribution 4.0.

By the early 1970s, basic education had spread in Ethiopia: Desta Asayehgn, "Socio-economic and Educational Reforms in Ethiopia (1942-1974): Correspondence and Contradiction," a report from UNESCO's International Institute for Educational

Planning, 1979.

Mago shelters an immense array of mammals and birds: Ethiopia Wildlife Conservation Authority, "Mago National Park Ten Years General Management Plan" published in 2019. The study cites effects on the park from the sugar plantation including the restricted mobility of animals due to the irrigation canal, and large animals falling into the waterway and dying, as well as decreased Omo River volume.

As so often happened in the Omo Valley, the trouble began in darkness: The account of the Hamar War and its aftermath is based on interviews with mediator Awoke Aike, South Omo Zone Chief Administrator Molloka Wubneh Toricha, and a Hamar elder, along with security situation reports at the time. Also valuable is the account of a policeman involved in the incident, in Yohannes Yitbarek, "Clashing Values: The 2015 Conflict in Hamar District of South Omo Zone, Southern Ethiopia," 381-383, in Susanne Epple and Getachew Assefa, editors, *Legal Pluralism in Ethiopia: Actors, Challenges and Solutions.*

Epilogue

On rare occasion, emissaries from the Omo slipped into that other world: The visit of Gulo and Dobi to supporters in Minnesota is recounted in a 2015 report by Global Team for Local Initiatives.

The Ethiopian planners had cut the size of the sugarcane

cultivation area: "FDRE Sugar Corporation Final Scoping Report," 1-8, in Government of Ethiopia, "Progress Report on the State of Conservation of the Lower Omo Valley Heritage Property," submitted to the director of the World Heritage Center on 30 January 2018.

One afternoon a voice, clear and familiar, issued from my phone: Interview with Molloka Wubneh Toricha, August 2021.

About the Author

Edward DeMarco was senior adviser for democracy and governance for the United States Agency for International Development in Ethiopia, where he led America's engagement on the development drama in the Lower Omo Valley. Later, in Zambia, he designed and launched one of America's largest democracy-support programs in sub-Saharan Africa. Before joining the United States Government, DeMarco was an international politics editor for Bloomberg in Washington. For his work on governance and human rights in Ethiopia, he received the Meritorious Honor Award from the Administrator of USAID.

United Nations Declaration on the Rights of Indigenous Peoples

Resolution adopted by the General Assembly
on 13 September 2007

The General Assembly,

Guided by the purposes and principles of the Charter of the United Nations, and good faith in the fulfilment of the obligations assumed by States in accordance with the Charter,

Affirming that indigenous peoples are equal to all other peoples, while recognizing the right of all peoples to be different, to consider themselves different, and to be respected as such,

Affirming also that all peoples contribute to the diversity and richness of civilizations and cultures, which constitute the common heritage of humankind,

Affirming further that all doctrines, policies and practices based on or advocating superiority of peoples or individuals on the basis of national origin or racial, religious, ethnic or cultural differences are racist, scientifically false, legally invalid, morally condemnable and socially unjust,

Reaffirming that indigenous peoples, in the exercise of their rights, should be free from discrimination of any kind,

Concerned that indigenous peoples have suffered from historic injustices as a result of, inter alia, their colonization and dispossession of their lands, territories and resources, thus preventing them from exercising, in particular, their right to development in accordance with their own needs and interests,

Recognizing the urgent need to respect and promote the inherent rights of indigenous peoples which derive from their political, economic and social structures and from their cultures, spiritual traditions, histories and philosophies, especially their rights to their lands, territories and resources,

Recognizing also the urgent need to respect and promote the rights of indigenous peoples affirmed in treaties, agreements and other constructive arrangements with States,

Welcoming the fact that indigenous peoples are organizing themselves for political, economic, social and cultural enhancement and in order to bring to an end all forms of discrimination and oppression wherever they occur,

Convinced that control by indigenous peoples over developments affecting them and their lands, territories and resources will enable them to maintain and strengthen their institutions, cultures and traditions, and to promote their development in accordance with their aspirations and needs,

Recognizing that respect for indigenous knowledge, cultures and traditional practices contributes to sustainable and equitable development and proper management of the environment,

Emphasizing the contribution of the demilitarization

of the lands and territories of indigenous peoples to peace, economic and social progress and development, understanding and friendly relations among nations and peoples of the world,

Recognizing in particular the right of indigenous families and communities to retain shared responsibility for the upbringing, training, education and well-being of their children, consistent with the rights of the child,

Considering that the rights affirmed in treaties, agreements and other constructive arrangements between States and indigenous peoples are, in some situations, matters of international concern, interest, responsibility and character,

Considering also that treaties, agreements and other constructive arrangements, and the relationship they represent, are the basis for a strengthened partnership between indigenous peoples and States,

Acknowledging that the Charter of the United Nations, the International Covenant on Economic, Social and Cultural Rights and the International

Covenant on Civil and Political Rights as well as the Vienna Declaration and Programme of Action, affirm the fundamental importance of the right to self-determination of all peoples, by virtue of which they freely determine their political status and freely pursue their economic, social and cultural development,

Bearing in mind that nothing in this Declaration may be used to deny any peoples their right to self-determination, exercised in conformity with international law,

Convinced that the recognition of the rights of indigenous peoples in this Declaration will enhance harmonious and cooperative relations between the State and indigenous peoples, based on principles of justice, democracy, respect for human rights, non-discrimination and good faith,

Encouraging States to comply with and effectively implement all their obligations as they apply to indigenous peoples under international instruments, in particular those related to human rights, in consultation and cooperation with the peoples concerned,

Emphasizing that the United Nations has an important and continuing role to play in promoting and protecting the rights of indigenous peoples,

Believing that this Declaration is a further important step forward for the recognition, promotion and protection of the rights and freedoms of indigenous peoples and in the development of relevant activities of the United Nations system in this field,

Recognizing and reaffirming that indigenous individuals are entitled without discrimination to all human rights recognized in international law, and that indigenous peoples possess collective rights which are indispensable for their existence, well-being and integral development as peoples,

Recognizing that the situation of indigenous peoples varies from region to region and from country to country and that the significance of national and regional particularities and various historical and cultural backgrounds should be taken into consideration,

Solemnly proclaims the following United Nations Declaration on the Rights of Indigenous Peoples as a standard of achievement to be pursued in a spirit of partnership and mutual respect:

Article 1

Indigenous peoples have the right to the full enjoyment, as a collective or as individuals, of all human rights and fundamental freedoms as recognized in the Charter of the United Nations, the Universal Declaration of Human Rights [4] and international human rights law.

Article 2

Indigenous peoples and individuals are free and equal to all other peoples and individuals and have the right to be free from any kind of discrimination, in the exercise of their rights, in particular that based on their indigenous origin or identity.

Article 3

Indigenous peoples have the right to self-determination. By virtue of that right they freely determine their political status and freely pursue their economic, social and cultural development.

Article 4

Indigenous peoples, in exercising their right to self-determination, have the right to autonomy or self-government in matters relating to their internal and local affairs, as well as ways and means for financing their autonomous functions.

Article 5

Indigenous peoples have the right to maintain and strengthen their distinct political, legal, economic, social and cultural institutions, while retaining their right to participate fully, if they so choose, in the political, economic, social and cultural life of the State.

Article 6

Every indigenous individual has the right to a nationality.

Article 7

1.   Indigenous individuals have the rights

to life, physical and mental integrity, liberty and security of person.

2. Indigenous peoples have the collective right to live in freedom, peace and security as distinct peoples and shall not be subjected to any act of genocide or any other act of violence, including forcibly removing children of the group to another group.

Article 8

1. Indigenous peoples and individuals have the right not to be subjected to forced assimilation or destruction of their culture.

2. States shall provide effective mechanisms for prevention of, and redress for:

(*a*) Any action which has the aim or effect of depriving them of their integrity as distinct peoples, or of their cultural values or ethnic identities;

(*b*) Any action which has the aim or effect of dispossessing them of their lands, territories or resources;

(*c*) Any form of forced population transfer which has the aim or effect of violating or undermining any of their rights;

(*d*) Any form of forced assimilation or integration;

(*e*) Any form of propaganda designed to promote or incite racial or ethnic discrimination directed against them.

Article 9

Indigenous peoples and individuals have the right to belong to an indigenous community or nation, in accordance with the traditions and customs of the community or nation concerned. No discrimination of any kind may arise from the exercise of such a right.

Article 10

Indigenous peoples shall not be forcibly removed from their lands or territories. No relocation shall take place without the free, prior and informed consent of the indigenous peoples concerned and after agreement on just and fair compensation and, where possible, with the option of return.

Article 11

1.   Indigenous peoples have the right to practise and revitalize their cultural traditions and customs. This includes the right to maintain, protect and develop the past, present and future manifestations of their cultures, such as archaeological and historical sites, artefacts, designs, ceremonies, technologies and visual and performing arts and literature.

2.   States shall provide redress through effective mechanisms, which may include restitution, developed in conjunction with indigenous peoples, with respect to their cultural, intellectual, religious and spiritual property taken without their free, prior and informed consent or in violation of their laws, traditions and customs.

Article 12

1.   Indigenous peoples have the right to manifest, practise, develop and teach their spiritual and religious traditions, customs and ceremonies; the right to maintain, protect, and have access in privacy to their religious and cultural sites; the right to the use and control of their ceremonial

objects; and the right to the repatriation of their human remains.

2.   States shall seek to enable the access and/ or repatriation of ceremonial objects and human remains in their possession through fair, transparent and effective mechanisms developed in conjunction with indigenous peoples concerned.

Article 13
1.   Indigenous peoples have the right to revitalize, use, develop and transmit to future generations their histories, languages, oral traditions, philosophies, writing systems and literatures, and to designate and retain their own names for communities, places and persons.

2.   States shall take effective measures to ensure that this right is protected and also to ensure that indigenous peoples can understand and be understood in political, legal and administrative proceedings, where necessary through the provision of interpretation or by other appropriate means.

Article 14

1.   Indigenous peoples have the right to establish and control their educational systems and institutions providing education in their own languages, in a manner appropriate to their cultural methods of teaching and learning.

2.   Indigenous individuals, particularly children, have the right to all levels and forms of education of the State without discrimination.

3.   States shall, in conjunction with indigenous peoples, take effective measures, in order for indigenous individuals, particularly children, including those living outside their communities, to have access, when possible, to an education in their own culture and provided in their own language.

Article 15

1.   Indigenous peoples have the right to the dignity and diversity of their cultures, traditions, histories and aspirations which shall be appropriately reflected in education and public information.2.   States shall take effective

measures, in consultation and cooperation with the indigenous peoples concerned, to combat prejudice and eliminate discrimination and to promote tolerance, understanding and good relations among indigenous peoples and all other segments of society.

Article 16

1. Indigenous peoples have the right to establish their own media in their own languages and to have access to all forms of non-indigenous media without discrimination.

2. States shall take effective measures to ensure that State-owned media duly reflect indigenous cultural diversity. States, without prejudice to ensuring full freedom of expression, should encourage privately owned media to adequately reflect indigenous cultural diversity.

Article 17

1. Indigenous individuals and peoples have the right to enjoy fully all rights established under applicable international and domestic labour law.

2. States shall in consultation and cooperation

with indigenous peoples take specific measures to protect indigenous children from economic exploitation and from performing any work that is likely to be hazardous or to interfere with the child's education, or to be harmful to the child's health or physical, mental, spiritual, moral or social development, taking into account their special vulnerability and the importance of education for their empowerment.

3. Indigenous individuals have the right not to be subjected to any discriminatory conditions of labour and, inter alia, employment or salary.

Article 18

Indigenous peoples have the right to participate in decision-making in matters which would affect their rights, through representatives chosen by themselves in accordance with their own procedures, as well as to maintain and develop their own indigenous decision-making institutions.

Article 19

States shall consult and cooperate in good faith with the indigenous peoples concerned through

their own representative institutions in order
to obtain their free, prior and informed consent
before adopting and implementing legislative or
administrative measures that may affect them.

Article 20

1.   Indigenous peoples have the right to maintain
and develop their political, economic and social
systems or institutions, to be secure in the
enjoyment of their own means of subsistence
and development, and to engage freely in all
their traditional and other economic activities.

2.   Indigenous peoples deprived of their means
of subsistence and development are entitled to
just and fair redress.

Article 21

1.   Indigenous peoples have the right, without
discrimination, to the improvement of their
economic and social conditions, including, inter
alia, in the areas of education, employment,
vocational training and retraining, housing,
sanitation, health and social security.

2.   States shall take effective measures and,

where appropriate, special measures to ensure continuing improvement of their economic and social conditions. Particular attention shall be paid to the rights and special needs of indigenous elders, women, youth, children and persons with disabilities.

Article 22

1. Particular attention shall be paid to the rights and special needs of indigenous elders, women, youth, children and persons with disabilities in the implementation of this Declaration.

2. States shall take measures, in conjunction with indigenous peoples, to ensure that indigenous women and children enjoy the full protection and guarantees against all forms of violence and discrimination.

Article 23

Indigenous peoples have the right to determine and develop priorities and strategies for exercising their right to development. In particular, indigenous peoples have the right to be actively involved in developing and determining health, housing and other economic and social programmes affecting them and, as far as possible, to administer such programmes through their own institutions.

Article 24

1. Indigenous peoples have the right to their traditional medicines and to maintain their health practices, including the conservation of their vital medicinal plants, animals and minerals. Indigenous individuals also have the right to access, without any discrimination, to all social and health services.

2. Indigenous individuals have an equal right to the enjoyment of the highest attainable standard of physical and mental health. States shall take the necessary steps with a view to achieving progressively the full realization of this right.

Article 25

Indigenous peoples have the right to maintain and strengthen their distinctive spiritual relationship with their traditionally owned or otherwise occupied and used lands, territories, waters and coastal seas and other resources and to uphold their responsibilities to future generations in this regard.

Article 26

1.   Indigenous peoples have the right to the lands, territories and resources which they have traditionally owned, occupied or otherwise used or acquired.

2.   Indigenous peoples have the right to own, use, develop and control the lands, territories and resources that they possess by reason of traditional ownership or other traditional occupation or use, as well as those which they have otherwise acquired.

3.   States shall give legal recognition and protection to these lands, territories and resources. Such recognition shall be conducted with due respect to the customs, traditions and land tenure systems of the indigenous peoples concerned.

Article 27

States shall establish and implement, in conjunction with indigenous peoples concerned, a fair, independent, impartial, open and transparent process, giving due recognition to indigenous peoples' laws, traditions, customs and land tenure systems, to recognize and adjudicate the rights of indigenous peoples pertaining to their lands, territories and resources, including those which were traditionally owned or otherwise occupied or used. Indigenous peoples shall have the right to participate in this process.

Article 28

1. Indigenous peoples have the right to redress, by means that can include restitution or, when this is not possible, just, fair and equitable compensation, for the lands, territories and resources which they have traditionally owned or otherwise occupied or used, and which have been confiscated, taken, occupied, used or damaged without their free, prior and informed consent.

2. Unless otherwise freely agreed upon by the peoples concerned, compensation shall take the form of lands, territories and resources equal in quality, size and legal status or of monetary compensation or other appropriate redress.

Article 29

1.   Indigenous peoples have the right to the conservation and protection of the environment and the productive capacity of their lands or territories and resources. States shall establish and implement assistance programmes for indigenous peoples for such conservation and protection, without discrimination.

2.   States shall take effective measures to ensure that no storage or disposal of hazardous materials shall take place in the lands or territories of indigenous peoples without their free, prior and informed consent.

3.   States shall also take effective measures to ensure, as needed, that programmes for monitoring, maintaining and restoring the health of indigenous peoples, as developed and implemented by the peoples affected by such materials, are duly implemented.

Article 30

1.   Military activities shall not take place in the lands or territories of indigenous peoples,

unless justified by a relevant public interest or otherwise freely agreed with or requested by the indigenous peoples concerned.

2. States shall undertake effective consultations with the indigenous peoples concerned, through appropriate procedures and in particular through their representative institutions, prior to using their lands or territories for military activities.

Article 31

1. Indigenous peoples have the right to maintain, control, protect and develop their cultural heritage, traditional knowledge and traditional cultural expressions, as well as the manifestations of their sciences, technologies and cultures, including human and genetic resources, seeds, medicines, knowledge of the properties of fauna and flora, oral traditions, literatures, designs, sports and traditional games and visual and performing arts. They also have the right to maintain, control, protect and develop their intellectual property over such cultural heritage, traditional knowledge, and traditional cultural expressions.

2.   In conjunction with indigenous peoples, States shall take effective measures to recognize and protect the exercise of these rights.

Article 32

1.   Indigenous peoples have the right to determine and develop priorities and strategies for the development or use of their lands or territories and other resources.

2.   States shall consult and cooperate in good faith with the indigenous peoples concerned through their own representative institutions in order to obtain their free and informed consent prior to the approval of any project affecting their lands or territories and other resources, particularly in connection with the development, utilization or exploitation of mineral, water or other resources.

3. States shall provide effective mechanisms for just and fair redress for any such activities, and appropriate measures shall be taken to mitigate adverse environmental, economic, social, cultural

or spiritual impact.

Article 33

1. Indigenous peoples have the right to determine their own identity or membership in accordance with their customs and traditions. This does not impair the right of indigenous individuals to obtain citizenship of the States in which they live.

2. Indigenous peoples have the right to determine the structures and to select the membership of their institutions in accordance with their own procedures.

Article 34

Indigenous peoples have the right to promote, develop and maintain their institutional structures and their distinctive customs, spirituality, traditions, procedures, practices and, in the cases where they exist, juridical systems or customs, in accordance with international human rights standards.

Article 35

Indigenous peoples have the right to determine the responsibilities of individuals to their communities.

Article 36

1.   Indigenous peoples, in particular those divided by international borders, have the right to maintain and develop contacts, relations and cooperation, including activities for spiritual, cultural, political, economic and social purposes, with their own members as well as other peoples across borders.

2.   States, in consultation and cooperation with indigenous peoples, shall take effective measures to facilitate the exercise and ensure the implementation of this right.

Article 37

1.   Indigenous peoples have the right to the recognition, observance and enforcement of treaties, agreements and other constructive arrangements concluded with States or their successors and to have States honour and respect such treaties, agreements and other constructive arrangements.

2. Nothing in this Declaration may be interpreted as diminishing or eliminating the rights of indigenous peoples contained in treaties, agreements and other constructive arrangements.

Article 38

States in consultation and cooperation with indigenous peoples, shall take the appropriate measures, including legislative measures, to achieve the ends of this Declaration.

Article 39

Indigenous peoples have the right to have access to financial and technical assistance from States and through international cooperation, for the enjoyment of the rights contained in this Declaration.

Article 40

Indigenous peoples have the right to access to and prompt decision through just and fair procedures for the resolution of conflicts and disputes with States or other parties, as well as to effective remedies for all infringements of their individual and collective rights. Such a decision shall give due consideration to the customs, traditions, rules and legal systems of the indigenous peoples concerned and international human rights.

Article 41

The organs and specialized agencies of the United Nations system and other intergovernmental organizations shall contribute to the full realization of the provisions of this Declaration through the mobilization, inter alia, of financial cooperation and technical assistance. Ways and means of ensuring participation of indigenous peoples on issues affecting them shall be established.

Article 42

The United Nations, its bodies, including the Permanent Forum on Indigenous Issues, and specialized agencies, including at the country level, and States shall promote respect for and full application of the provisions of this Declaration and follow up the effectiveness of this Declaration.

Article 43

The rights recognized herein constitute the minimum standards for the survival, dignity and well-being of the indigenous peoples of the world.

Article 44

All the rights and freedoms recognized herein are equally guaranteed to male and female indigenous individuals.

Article 45

Nothing in this Declaration may be construed as diminishing or extinguishing the rights indigenous peoples have now or may acquire in the future.

Article 46

1. Nothing in this Declaration may be interpreted as implying for any State, people, group or person any right to engage in any activity or to perform any act contrary to the Charter of the United Nations or construed as authorizing or encouraging any action which would dismember or impair, totally or in part, the territorial integrity or political unity of sovereign and independent

States.

2.   In the exercise of the rights enunciated in the present Declaration, human rights and fundamental freedoms of all shall be respected. The exercise of the rights set forth in this Declaration shall be subject only to such limitations as are determined by law and in accordance with international human rights obligations. Any such limitations shall be non-discriminatory and strictly necessary solely for the purpose of securing due recognition and respect for the rights and freedoms of others and for meeting the just and most compelling requirements of a democratic society.

3.   The provisions set forth in this Declaration shall be interpreted in accordance with the principles of justice, democracy, respect for human rights, equality, non-discrimination, good governance and good faith.

www.ingramcontent.com/pod-product-compliance
Lightning Source LLC
Chambersburg PA
CBHW060450280326
41933CB00014B/2720